When You Catch an Adjective, Kill It

The Sound on the Page: Style and Voice in Writing

About Town: The New Yorker *and the World It Made*

Will Rogers: A Biography

The Art of Fact: A Historical Anthology of Literary Journalism
    (co-editor)

.

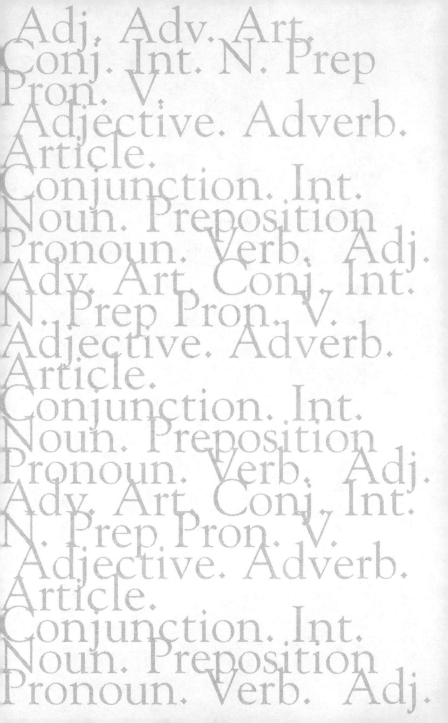

When You Catch an Adjective, Kill It

THE PARTS OF SPEECH,

FOR BETTER

AND/OR WORSE

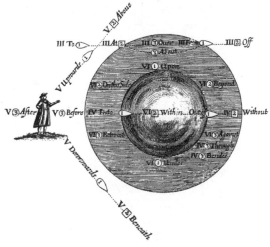

Ben Yagoda

Broadway Books

New York

PUBLISHED BY BROADWAY BOOKS

Published in the United States by Broadway Books, an imprint of The
Doubleday Broadway Publishing Group, a division of
Random House, Inc., New York.
www.broadwaybooks.com

BROADWAY BOOKS and its logo, a letter B bisected on the diagonal,
are trademarks of Random House, Inc.

Title page illustration taken from *An Essay Towards a Real Character, and a
Philosophical Language* by John Wilkins (1668).
Lyrics on page 100 taken from "Moments in the Woods," words and music
by Stephen Sondheim © 1987, 1988, 1989, Rilting Music, Inc. All Rights
Administered by WB Music Corp. All Rights Reserved. Used by permission.

Library of Congress Cataloging-in-Publication Data
Yagoda, Ben.
     When you catch an adjective, kill it : The parts of speech, for better
and/or worse / Ben Yagoda.— 1st ed.
          p.   cm.
     1.   English language—Parts of speech.   2.   English language—
Syntax.   3.   English language—Grammar.   4.   Vocabulary.   I.   Title.
PE1199.H33 2006
425'.5—dc22
                                                            2006040547

ISBN-13: 978-0-7679-2077-3
ISBN-10: 0-7679-2077-5

PRINTED IN THE UNITED STATES OF AMERICA

10 9 8 7 6 5 4

To Elizabeth Yagoda and Maria Yagoda

my ears on the ground

contents

ack**acknowledgments**

The leadoff spot has to go to Geoffrey Pullum, who un-
accountably took an interest in this project and sent me
many patient, learned, and extremely helpful e-mails
containing sentences like "In considering 'so,' we need
to appreciate that it can be either a 'subordinating conjunction' of the sort that we prefer to treat as a clause-
taking preposition, or a coordinator." Jocelyn Jones and
Tarra Avis were outstanding research assistants. Making
diverse and much-appreciated contributions were Bruce
Beans, Mark Bowden, Susan Brynteson, Tim Burke,
John Caskey, Wes Davis, David Friedman, Bo Goldman, Paul Gluck, John Grossmann, Denis Harper, Jim
Hazard, Steve Helmling, Ron Javers, John Jebb, McKay
Jenkins, Eliot Kaplan, Erick Kelleman, Kevin Kerrane,
Ralph Keyes, Mike Kolatch, Don Lessem, Mark Liber-
man, Donald Mell, Taki Michaelidis, Chris Mills,
Lazaros Molho, John Morse, Shaun Mullen, Steven
Pinker, Lois Potter, Charles Robinson, Gil Rose, Chip
Scanlan, Rick Selvin, Allan Siegal, Margaret Y. Sime-
one, Bill Stempel, Danny Sullivan, Lizzie Terry, Rick

Valelly, Bob Zaglin, and Arnold Zwicky. The English department at the University of Delaware, chaired by Jerry Beasley and Steve Bernhardt, is a hospitable home base. Stuart Krichevsky picks the very best on-hold music, and Kris Puopolo had me at ampersand. That Gigi Simeone and Elizabeth and Maria Yagoda love language is only one of the reasons I love them.

When You Catch an Adjective, Kill It

introduction

In the end, it came down to two potential titles. Number one, *When You Catch an Adjective, Kill It.* Number two, *Pimp My Ride.* I have to admit that I carry a torch for number two—which alludes, of course, to the popular MTV series in which a posse of automotive artisans take a run-down jalopy and sleek it up into an awe-inspiring vehicle containing many square yards of plush velvet and an astonishing number of LCD screens. Leaving aside the fact that it would have lent a faint aura of hipness to a book otherwise sorely lacking in street cred, *Pimp My Ride* illustrates a deep and wonderful truth about the parts of speech: they change like the dickens. *Pimp*—a noun meaning a procurer of prostitutes—turns into a transitive verb, meaning, roughly, "to make pimp-worthy." And the intransitive verb *ride* becomes a noun, meaning that in which one rides.

The nineteenth-century philosopher John Stuart Mill holds out a temptingly lofty rationale for a consideration of the parts of speech, claiming that they represent fundamental categories of human thought. This is an attractive notion for any parts-of-speech fan, and certainly for someone (i.e., me) who has just devoted 2.7 percent of his life to the subject, but ultimately it doesn't hold water. For one thing, you find strikingly different systems in other languages, such as Latin and Korean, neither of which contains adjectives as a distinct class. (In Latin, you express the quality of a thing with nouns, and in Korean with verbs.) For another, even within a particular tradition, the lineup of categories keeps shifting. Writing in about 100 B.C.E., the Greek grammarian Thrax, who invented the whole idea of parts of speech, counted eight of them: adverbs, articles, conjunctions, nouns, participles, prepositions, pronouns, and verbs. The Romans had to drop articles (that is, *a* and *the*), since such words didn't exist in Latin, and added—hot damn!—interjections. The early English grammarians started out by adopting the Latin scheme, and it wasn't until Joseph Priestley's *The Rudiments of English Grammar*, published in 1761, that someone came up with the familiar baseball-team-sized list that included adjectives and booted out participles for good. This is the list that most of us remember from grammar school, that people who were kids in the 1970s remember from the ABC series *Schoolhouse Rock!* (and who could forget the classic song "Conjunction Junction [what's your function?]"), and that I adopt here.

Broadly speaking, there are two groups of people who think, talk, and write a lot about language, and the parts of speech give both of them *agita*. The "prescriptivists," language commentators of the Edwin Newman/John Simon/Lynne Truss school, peer at something like *Pimp My Ride* and see the decline of Western civilization. The process in which nouns like *impact* and *access*, or a noun phrase like *fast track*, are verbed is called "functional shifting." These shifts are indeed lame in a stiff bureaucraticky way, and Alexander Haig did indeed butcher the language when he said things like "I'll have to *caveat* any response, Senator"; "Not the way you *contexted* it, Senator"; and "There are *nuanceal* differences between Henry Kissinger and me on that."

But shifting has been going on for a long, long time. In the words of Garland Cannon, the author of *Historical Change and English Word-Formation*, the process became "productive in Middle English, when the nouns *duke* and *lord* acquired verb functions, the verbs *cut* and *rule* shifted to a noun." Shakespeare was the past master of this kind of thing; he had characters say "*season* your admiration," "*dog* them at the heels," "*backing* a horse," plus *elbow*, *drug*, *gossip*, *lapse*, and *silence*—none of them ever used before as verbs.

Nouns still get verbed every day, much to the despair

of the prescriptivists. A very successful recent shift is that of the trade name Google from proper noun to a transitive verb meaning "to look up in an Internet search engine." Google, the company, doesn't fancy this either. In his book *Word Spy*, Paul McFedries writes that "violators are sent a polite note along with a document outlining some 'examples of appropriate and inappropriate uses of Google's trademark.' " An appropriate use, according to the company, would be: "I used Google to check out that guy I met at the party." And an inappropriate one: "I Googled that hottie."

Lots of other parts of speech can shift, too. Consider:

I was having a real fun time until I totaled my car, which was a rare make, a quality ride, and a collectible. Shoot! Then my parents started to guilt me. The whole thing weirded me out so bad that I couldn't stop goddamming. I know it's totally cliché, but I had to down a Scotch.

Real, *bad*: adjective to adverb. *Fun*, *quality*: noun to adjective. *Totaled*, *weirded*: adjective to verb. *Make*, *ride*: verb to noun. *Guilt*: noun to verb. *Collectible*, *Scotch*: adjective to noun. *Cliché*: noun to adjective. *Shoot*: verb to interjection. *Goddamming*: interjection to verb. *Down*: adverb to verb.

The real fun starts when a word shifts more than once. *Frame* started as a verb, meaning "to form," then became a noun meaning "border," and emerged as a new verb meaning "to put a frame *around* something." In a similar way, the noun *wire* engendered a verb ("I wired him the news") and from that turned into another noun ("He sent me a wire"). Despite being less than two centuries old, *okay* is commonly used as five different parts of speech: adjective ("It was an okay movie"), adverb ("The team played okay"), interjection ("Okay!"), noun ("The boss gave her okay"), and verb ("The president okayed the project").

Especially in the realm of slang, the changes can be dizzying. The English newspaper *The Guardian* ran an item quoting a line from a novel called *Afterburn* by a writer called Zane: "No matter how hoochie I tried to be, she out-hoochied me every time." Noting that the book was about to be issued in Japan, *The Guardian* took public pity on its translator.

Sometimes this process goes in reverse. In 1897, James Murray, the founding editor of the *Oxford English Dictionary* (*OED*), was obliged to write a definition for *burgle*, which had appeared in print for the very first time just twenty-six years earlier and had gained popularity since. Murray surmised that the originator had shortened the old words *burglar* and *burglary* to create the verb, and he coined the term *back-formation* to describe the process. Other back-formations generally follow the *burgle* model and create verbs; they include *edit* from *editor*, *televise* from *television*, *baby-sit* from *baby-sitter*, *diagnose* from *diagnosis*, *laze* from *lazy*, *beg* from *beggar*, *type* from *typewriter*, *donate* from *donation*, *emote* from *emotion*, and *grovel* from the adjective *groveling*. (Shakespeare came up with that one.) *Greed* is a noun formed from the adjective *greedy*, and *difficult* an adjective formed from the noun *difficulty*. Of course, some attempted back-formations aren't as successful as the foregoing. A group of therapists once tried to float the verb *therap*; *enthuse* is pretty iffy; and English drawing-room comedies always get a laugh at the expense of someone who describes the occupation of the guy dressed in black as *buttling*.

I'm with the prescriptivists on *enthuse*. By contrast, the "descriptivists"—the other group that obsesses about language—would go to their deaths defending the use of *hopefully* to mean "it is to be hoped that" simply because people *use it that way*. These are the linguists and academic grammarians whose motto, borrowed from Alexander Pope, is "Whatever is, is right." The descriptivists don't like the parts of speech either, because they're so, well, inexact. As far back as 1924, the great grammarian Otto Jespersen rather wryly remarked of them, "The definitions are very far from having attained the degree of exactitude found in Euclidean geometry." Writing at about the same time, Edward Sapir was more direct: "No logical scheme of the parts of speech— their number, nature, and necessary confines—is of the slightest interest to the linguist." In truth, any parts-of-speech scheme leaves gaping holes. In the term *baseball player* is the word *baseball* a noun or an adjective? Reasonable people differ on this point. What about the word *to* in an infinitive like *to see*, what about the *there* in *there are*, what about numbers? If you're looking for definitive answers, you'll be looking for a long time.

Recent scholars have gone so far as to reject the very *term* "parts of speech" in favor of proxies like "word classes" and "lexical categories." A useful recent trend has been to accept the "fuzziness" of the categories, whatever you call them. The prolific writer on language David Crystal notes, "Modern grammars recognize that the largest word classes are convenient fictions, to some degree." Nouns, for instance, are often defined by having some or all of a list of features. Most notably: they can be the subject or object of a sentence or clause; they can have a plural form; they can display a suffix such as *-ish* or *-hood*. A word like *mother*, which does all three things, is thus a very "nouny" noun. *Paris*, which satisfies only the first criterion, is on the fringes of the category.

Me, I like the parts of speech. One way to explain why is with a story about Harold Ross, the legendary founding editor of *The New Yorker* magazine. Among quite a few other things, Ross was obsessed with articles—the grammatical rather than the journalistic kind. For several decades, he ran a sort of one-man crusade against the word *the*, which he maintained should be used only to introduce a noun or noun phrase designating a unique entity. His position is not really tenable. We would say "I answered the phone" even if there were a half dozen extensions in the house, and we say "I went to the doctor" despite there being millions of M.D.s on the planet. But Ross's mania about the word went beyond logic, as manias tend to do.

It was all tied up in his feelings about a stylistic offense he called "indirection." This, his colleague Wolcott Gibbs explained in a 1937 memo titled "The Theory and Practice of Editing *New Yorker* Articles,"

> probably maddens Mr. Ross more than anything in the world. He objects, that is, to important objects being dragged into things in a secretive and underhanded manner. If, for instance, a profile has never told where a man lives, Ross protests against a sentence saying, "His Vermont house is full of valuable

paintings." Should say "He has a house in Vermont and it is full, etc."

The word *the*, in Ross's eyes, was the principal perpetrator of indirection; references to "the car," "the man," or "the overcoat" in a piece of writing were unacceptable unless the existence of said car, man, and coat had been previously established. Once, S. J. Perelman submitted to *The New Yorker* a humor piece that referred to "the woman taken in adultery," without spelling out that this was a reference to John 8:3. Ross, not a devout man, penciled a query in the margin: "*What* woman?"

In the late 1940s, a not-yet-famous Russian émigré writer named Vladimir Nabokov began submitting to *The New Yorker* a series of autobiographical essays. One of them, "Lantern Slides," concluded with a kind of montage of scenes of his youth in St. Petersburg. Nabokov wrote about the moment when

a torrent of sounds come to life: voices speaking all together, a walnut cracked, the click of the nutcracker carelessly passed, thirty human hearts drowning mine with their regular beats.

Harold Ross was famous for queries such as the one he laid on Perelman—comments and questions he would scribble in the margins of *New Yorker* stories being readied for publication. The most celebrated, which Ross would insert whenever he felt a person was named but insufficiently identified, was "Who he?" On Nabokov's galleys he circled the *the* that came before the word *nutcracker* and wrote in the margin: "Were the Nabokovs a *one*-nutcracker family?" This mystified the author. His editor, Katharine White, explained Ross's point: if in fact the family owned more than one such utensil, Ross was suggesting that the word *a* be substituted for *the*.

So here's why I'm keen on the parts of speech: you cannot understand the difference between *a nutcracker* and *the nutcracker*—and a momentous difference it is— unless you're attentive enough to language to understand just what an article is. And the same goes for a thousand other examples. As the anonymous author of a 1733 book called *The English Accidence* put it, the parts of speech are "the foundation upon which the beautiful fabrick of the language stands."

I like that he or she used the word *beautiful*. Prescriptivists and descriptivists alike have recently sent forth a profusion of essays, books, and other volleys in the language wars, but they all seem to lack a sense of the beauty, the joy, the artistry, and the fun of English. The prescriptivists' case is weakened, in addition, by the simple and unassailable fact that language changes. One example: A couple of generations ago, every grammar-school grammar teacher drilled into her charges' heads the eternal rule that one forms the future tense in the first person by using the auxiliary verb *shall*. Today, the only possible response to anyone who says, "I shall go to the store" is "And I shall call you a dork till the end of your days."

The main flaw of the descriptivists is their own inconsistency. People such as Harvard psychologist Steven Pinker—whose book *The Language Instinct* contains a chapter roundly ripping the "language mavens"—and the editors of the jaw-droppingly comprehensive *Merriam-Webster's Dictionary of English Usage* put forth an it's-all-good philosophy, yet in their own writing *follow all the traditional rules*. That is, as much as he defends it, you won't catch Pinker using *hopefully*. This school underestimates the difference in protocol between speaking and writing, unjustifiably applying the inherent looseness of the one to the necessary (to some extent) formality of the other.

Ultimately, the issue of correctness just isn't very interesting. Given the inevitability of change, the only question is how long a shift in spelling, syntax, punctuation, semantics, or any other aspect of usage should be in popular use before it becomes standard or accepted.

Some people want things to move fast, some people want things to move slow (except they would say *slowly*), and none of them has much of an impact on the actual rate of change.

I realized some time ago that I have a tendency to divide all experience—buildings, people, movies, songs, weather, roads, hamburgers—into two categories. The first category makes me happy to be alive. The other category makes me sad, or at best neutral. And, in the realm of language, *that's* the kind of Manichaean division I care about, and that you'll find throughout this book. In taking such an approach I'm inspired by two earlier books, both published in the first decades of the twentieth century. One is more or less descriptivist, one is more or less prescriptivist, neither is subject to the extremism of today's language ideologues, and both are governed by the idea that language artfully used can make you happy to be alive.

The first is H. L. Mencken's *The American Language*, which he initially published in 1919 and kept adding on to for the next thirty years. Mencken catalogued the slang, neologisms, place names, and wacky spelling and pronunciation of his countrymen out of pure anthropological zeal; his enthusiasm seeps from his pages and makes the book still a pleasure to read today. His influence lives in all kinds of interesting and cool investigations: for example, a body of scholarship (described in Chapter VIII of this book) dedicated to finding out whether the Southern second-person pronoun y'*all* is or isn't exclusively plural. The other book is the 1926 *Modern English Usage*, otherwise known as "Fowler's," after its author, Henry W.; it was invisibly revised (that's a good thing) by Sir Ernest Gowers in 1965, and quite visibly so by Robert Burchfield in 1996. Fowler is almost completely unconcerned with "right" and "wrong." What he cares about, in such classic entries as "Elegant Variation"—which eviscerates the figure of speech, still thriving on ESPN, by which a ballplayer is referred to as "the fleet-footed second-sacker"—is good usage and bad.

So what do *I* consider bad? Horrible clichés like "the language wars" (used by yours truly five paragraphs above, and permitted to remain in the text only to provide an object lesson), mind-numbing phrasing like "Not the way you contexted it, Senator," and, sure, *hopefully*. I dislike *hopefully* not because it's wrong—check out Chapter II for an explanation of its kosherness—but because people who use it in writing tend to be imprecise, muddy, solipsistic, and dull.

And what makes me happy to be a living utilizer of English? Words, phrases, and sentences that transcend their meaning—because they're smart, funny, well-crafted, pungent, unexpected, or sometimes wrong in just the right way. (It's no coincidence that the majority of *Bartlett's Familiar Quotations* taken from speech rather than writing aren't grammatical. Two of them come from one man, boxing trainer Joe Jacobs: "We was robbed" and "I should of stood in bed.") You'll find examples on just about every page of this book, and in fact you've already encountered "pimp my ride," "she out-hoochied me every time," "Who he?," and "Were the Nabokovs a *one*-nutcracker family?"

And by the way, it turns out they weren't. One of the charming things about Harold Ross's queries was that they were precisely that; he was proud of the *New Yorker* tradition of never imposing an editorial change on an author. Nabokov decided that he preferred the original *the*, and his essay appeared with it in the February 11, 1950, issue of the magazine. But here is the kicker. Nabokov collected his reminiscences in 1966, in a book entitled *Speak, Memory*. During the interim, he'd apparently thought a good deal about Ross's question, for at the end of the ninth chapter, after the mentions of the torrents of sound and the voices speaking all together and the cracking of a walnut, there are these words: "the click of a nutcracker carelessly passed."

CHAPTER I

Adj.

Adv. Art.
Conj. Int. N.
Prep. Pron. V.

Look to the adjectives.
—*Virgil Thomson*

Kicking things off with adjectives is a little like starting a kids' birthday party with the broccoli course. Because as far as not getting respect goes, adjectives leave Rodney Dangerfield in the dust. They rank right up there with Osama bin Laden, Geraldo Rivera, and the customer-service policies of cable TV companies. That it is good to avoid them is one of the few points on which the sages of writing agree. Thus Voltaire: "The adjective is the enemy of the noun." Thus William Zinsser: "Most adjectives are . . . unnecessary. Like adverbs, they are sprinkled into sentences by writers who don't stop to think that the concept is already in the noun."

And thus the title of this book, a piece of advice traditionally attributed to Mark Twain.

Even the ancient Greeks seem to have been dismissive

of the adjective; their term for it was *epitheto*, meaning "something thrown on." In Latin, as previously noted, there *are* no adjectives as such, and such was the influence of that ancient language that the earlier English grammarians categorized these words as a subset of nouns. In 1735, John Collyer sensibly objected:

> Words that signify the Quality of the Thing, cannot come under the same Denomination with those that signify the Name of the Thing; And seeing the Adverb, which signifies the Manner of the Verb is made a distinct Part of Speech, why should not the Adjective be so too, since it bears at least the same relation to the Noun, as that doth the Verb?

His reasoning could not really be disputed, and not long afterward the adjective became a full-fledged part of speech. The situation is not quite as simple as Collyer made it out, however. For one thing, "words that signify the Quality of the Thing," as he puts it, come from a lot of different sources. There are not only the run-of-the-mill adjectives like *good*, *bad*, and *ugly*, but also various verb forms (a *driving* rain, a *decorated* cake); words created from suffixes like *-ific*, *-ive*, *-ous*, *-ful*, *-less*, and *-ic*; words that do double duty as nouns and adjectives (*green*); both cardinal (*two*) and ordinal (*second*) numbers; determiners or possessive pronouns like *the*, *those*, and *my*; hyphenated adjective phrases such as *high-quality*; and so-called attributive nouns, such as the first word in the phrases *company man*, *wedding cake*, and *motel room*.

Not all of these make the grade as full-fledged adjectives. One fairly reliable test is whether a word can be modified by an adverb—for example, *very*, *almost*, or *absolutely*. Colors certainly qualify and numbers are usually seen as doing so as well; we could say, "Susie is almost three." But *the*, *those*, *my*, *company*, *wedding*, and *motel* (in the above examples) are not adjectives, despite the fact that they modify or describe nouns. Some words edge their way into the class over time, at which point they are looked down on by usage commentators. A classic example is *fun*, which started out as an attributive noun, in such phrases as *fun house* (in the circus) and Mayor John Lindsay's much-mocked description of New York, *Fun City*. Fun was not a quality of the house or the city; the idea, rather, was that in these places one had fun (a noun). In the years since then, *fun* has stepped out into the footlights as an adjective, sparingly at first and now robustly. So you see and hear it modified by *very* and *so*, and used in comparative form as *funner* and *funnest*. (*Key* is traveling a similar road.) Journalist Barbara Wallraff quoted

Steven Pinker as saying that he "can tell whether people are over thirty years old or under by whether they're willing to accept *fun* as a full-fledged adjective." I'm well over thirty but have no objection to *fun* being used this way, at least in speech. After all, the only alternative for "That was a really fun trip" is "That was a really enjoyable trip," which is the kind of thing Eddie Haskell would say.

But, to reiterate, I am not one of those whatever-is-is-right loose constructionists; some new adjectives make me Sad to Be Alive. When someone says, "That's very cliché," my reaction is "That's very icky." *Clichéd* is a perfectly good adjective that was already in the dictionary. Equally grating is the shortening of the phrasal adjective *high-quality* to just plain *quality*, as in "He's a quality individual." Unfortunately, the trend is clearly going the other way: a Yahoo search for the phrase *a quality individual* yields more than 15,200 hits.

While we're on the subject of Pinker's "language mavens," here's their number one adjective-related complaint: the use of comparative or intensifying modifiers with supposedly "absolute" adjectives. The poster child here is *unique*. How would grammar geeks and English teachers spend their time if they were prohibited from tsk-tsking at *more unique* and *very unique*, or explaining that since unique means one-of-a-kind, there can be no degrees of uniqueness? But the mavens' kvetching on this point won't wash. The *OED* notes that since the nineteenth century, *unique* "has been in very common use, with a tendency to take the wider meaning of 'uncommon, unusual, remarkable.' " The dictionary quotes Kenneth Grahame's 1908 *The Wind in the Willows*: " 'Toad Hall,' said the Toad proudly, 'is an eligible self-contained gentleman's residence, very unique.' " Other absolutes can profitably be modified as well. Orwell expressed his point perfectly when he wrote in *Animal Farm*, "All animals are equal, but some animals are more equal than others." And the framers of the U.S. Constitution knew exactly what they were doing when they wrote, "We the People of the United States, in order to form a more perfect union . . ."

There are two main kinds of adjectives: attributive ones normally come right before the noun they qualify, while predicative adjectives come after *to be* or similar verbs such as *become* and *seem*. Most adjectives can serve either purpose: we can speak of a "happy family" and say "the family appeared happy." But some work only one way. Take the sentence "Clergymen are *answerable* to a *higher* authority." *Answerable* is exclusively a predicative; you could not refer to an "answerable clergyman." And *higher* is strictly attributive; you wouldn't normally say, "The authority is higher."

Attributive adjectives sometimes follow the model of French and come after the noun, as when we refer to accounts *payable*, something *important*, proof *positive*, matters *philosophical*, paradise *lost*, a battle *royal*, the heir *apparent*, stage *left*, time *immemorial*, or a Miller *Lite*. And predicative adjectives appear before the noun when used appositively: "*Tall*, *dark*, and *homely*, he is a natural choice to play the part of Abraham Lincoln."

That brings up another wrinkle. Attributive and predicative adjectives can both be listed in a series, but they behave in different ways. In normal usage, predicative ones are separated by a comma and the last item is preceded by a conjunction, usually *and*, *but*, *or*, or *yet*: for example, in the title of Lorraine Hansberry's play *To Be Young, Gifted and Black* or in the lyric "Three cheers for the red, white, and blue." Attributive lists can conclude with a conjunction ("The stuffed, stamped, and sealed envelopes go on the table") or not ("The quick, brown fox jumps over the lazy dog"; "Stately, plump Buck Mulligan"—the first four words of *Ulysses*). The comma issue opens a can of worms. Some people have an instinctive sense of it. They are the lucky ones. The logic behind the usage, basically, is that if adjectives qualify a noun in the same way, and if their order can be changed without doing any damage to the sentence, they should be separated by commas: "We had to cross a *wide*, *rough*, *freezing* river." On the other hand, you don't put commas between adjectives that modify each other or before ones that are part a noun phrase: "We stayed at a *luxurious seaside* motel"; "He is the *second happy married enlisted* man I've talked to today." Sometimes there's a mix: "Tiger Woods was the first righthanded [comma] browneyed [no comma] American golfer to win the tournament."* The trusty trick you might remember from junior high school still works: if inserting an *and* between any pair of adjectives in the series sounds okay, use a comma. If not, don't.

Now you know what adjectives are, but you may still be wondering why so many people bash them. These words are clearly necessary in order to communicate many thoughts and ideas: how could we make our way in the world without saying things like the "other cup," an "old man," the "green door," the "last day," etc., etc.? Moreover, adjectives aren't really used that much—they account for only about 6 percent of all words in the British National Corpus, a 100-million-word collection

---

* The very complicated rules for determining the order of such adjectives are, praise God, beyond the scope of this book. But note how in the second example, you could not change the order of any of the words in the series without making it into nonsense.

of samples of written and spoken language. The root of the problem is lazy writers' inordinate fondness for this part of speech. They start hurling the epithets when they haven't provided enough data—specific nouns and active verbs—to get their idea across. It's easy—too easy—to describe a woman as "beautiful." It takes more heavy verbal lifting, but is more effective, to point out that the jaw of every male in the room dropped when she walked in. And establishing that someone kicked an opponent who was down, stole seventeen dollars from a Salvation Army collection kettle, and lied to partners about having sexually transmitted diseases precludes the need to call him terrible, awful, horrible, horrid, deplorable, despicable, or vile.

Describing nature may be writers' toughest challenge—and many face it by stacking up the attributive adjectives, with a sprinkling of adverbs. An adherence to this formula may in fact be the most reliable sign of bad poetry: each line seems like an unfunny game of Mad-Libs. "The ____ snow fell ____ on the ____ ground as the ____ children played ____."

adj.   adv.   adj.   adj.   adv.

Generally speaking, it's the attributive adjectives that are abused; the predicative ones, coming after a verb, tend to encourage more thought and selectivity. Certainly, attributive adjectives are a feature of clichés and catchphrases. Have you recently heard of a bystander who wasn't innocent, a lining that wasn't silver, or a break that wasn't lucky? This isn't a new thing, either. In his 1930 book *Adjectives—and Other Words*, Ernest Weekley noted that after an assassination attempt on Mussolini, "the President of the Irish Free State congratulated him on 'providential escape' from 'odious attack,' sent his 'earnest wishes' for a 'speedy recovery' from the 'infamous attempt' that had caused 'utmost indignation,' etc." "There are people," Weekley observed, "who seem to think that a noun unaccompanied by an adjective has no real signification." A line of journalism quoted by Fowler in *Modern English Usage*— "The operation needs considerable skill and should be performed with proper care"—illustrates the point. The adjectives *considerable* and *proper* not only are unnecessary; they actually weaken the writer's point. Yet one can understand the impulse to put them in, for it has been felt by all of us.

Finally, when writers commit the sin of showing off— of being flowery or obscure for no reason other than to call attention to themselves—more often than not the tools of the crime are NOAs (needlessly obscure adjectives). There is no reason to use *rebarbative* instead of *unpleasant*, *annoying*, or some other familiar negative epithet, other than to be fancy. (A glossary at the end of the chapter defines *rebarbative* and all the other unfamil-

iar adjectives mentioned.) T. S. Eliot made a fetish of using long-dormant adjectives like *defunctive*, *anfractuous*,
and *polyphiloprogenetive*; he apparently felt *piacular*
(meaning something done or offered in order to make up
for a sin or sacrilegious action) was too run-of-the-mill,
so he made up a new form: *piaculative*. Senator Robert
Byrd is justly snickered at for saying things like "maledicent language" and "contumelious lip." Gore Vidal
has been accused of excessive fondness for words like
mephitic and *riparian*. In just one essay, James Fenton
writes, "The element of the aleatoric may well be gen-
uinely present," and refers to "proleptic writers such as
Ibsen and Strindberg" and to a "hieratic figure somewhat
reminiscent of Ernst." That's too proleptic for me.

The best use for this kind of adjective is comedy. In
One Fat Englishman, Kingsley Amis's narrator expresses
surprise that the cast of characters in a young American's
novel does not include "paraplegic necrophiles, hippoerotic jockeys, exhibitionistic castrates, coprophagic
pig-farmers, armless flagellationists and the rest of the
bunch." S. J. Perelman made a career out of formulations
such as "the evening a young person from the Garrick
Gaeities, in a corybantic mood, swung into a cancan and
executed a kick worthy of La Goulue."

But some writers' abuse of adjectives has led to the
defamation of an entire part of speech. A resourceful

and creative use of these words marks, more than any other single trait, a first-rate essayist or critic. It's an indication of originality, wit, observation—the cast and quality of the writer's mind. As Herbert Read writes in *English Prose Style*:

> The necessity of epithets can be determined by a nice judgment, but to use them appropriately is to employ a more instinctive faculty. In simple cases there is no choice: the meaning to be expressed demands one epithet and no other. But in other cases an unusual epithet must be sought to express a subtlety of feeling. . . . The free use of epithets is a characteristic of a mature literature, of highly developed civilizations and analytical minds.

I agree—so strongly that I'll admit, at the risk of being called a train-spotter, that I have been collecting outstanding or notable examples of adjective use for close to two decades. What can I tell you? It floats my boat. A recent addition to my thick file is a sentence from an op-ed piece the novelist William Boyd wrote for the *New York Times*. Talking of French TV weather people's dour forecasts about the hot summer, he wrote, "The tone is minatory and worrying, and very infectious." *Worrying* and *infectious* are good, but what made me clip the quote was *minatory*, which I found defined in the dictionary as "menacing or threatening." So why is it better than *menacing* or *threatening*? Well, the *-ing* ending of either would awkwardly echo *worrying* (itself a nice adj.), as well as incorrectly imply that the weathercasters themselves embodied a threat.

I didn't mind looking up *minatory* in the dictionary. That book contains some really good adjectives whose meanings more familiar ones simply can't get at. Simple words are fine for broad brushstrokes but often not adequate for the intricacies and fine points and nuances of human relationships, characteristics, and situations. Nor is it necessary to carry *Webster's* with you at all times. When these words are deployed skillfully, a reader can often infer or at least guess at the meaning from the context. Here are some nice examples, from my files, of the unfamiliar adj.:

"In those trusses I saw a reminder of a country-fairgrounds grandstand, or perhaps the *penumbrous* bones of the Polo Grounds roof." —Roger Angell on the gridwork at the new baseball stadium in Baltimore

"She shook her head, and a smell of *alembicated* summer touched his nostrils." —Sylvia Townsend Warner

"The Sunday's events repeated themselves in his mind, bending like *nacreous* flakes around a central *infrangible* irritant." —John Updike

"He had the surface involvement—style—while I had the deep-structural, immobilizing *synovial* ballooning of a superior mind." —Nicholson Baker on Updike

"The great out-sticking ears that frame his face like *cartilaginous* quotation marks." —Michael Kelly on Ross Perot

"Churchill is morally *irrefrangible* in American discourse, and can be quoted even more safely than Lincoln." —Christopher Hitchens

". . . the *chordal* quality of a man who is simultaneously overbearing and winning." —Stanley Kauffmann

". . . a *fissiparous*, splintered artifact." —Alex Clark on Ali Smith's novel *The Accidental*

Some other nifty uncommon adjectives I've collected are *mordant, factitious, sentient, supererogatory, capacious, supercilious, sedulous, fustian, captious, supernal, noisome, baleful, phatic, liminal, nugatory, tensile, cumbrous, perdurable, refulgent, anodyne, tenebrous, bibulous, gormless, shambolic, panoptic, otiose, oneiric, bumptious, demotic, pharaonic, pertinacious,* and *ludic.*

Much of this is a matter of taste, to be sure. The words listed above work for me; you may find them show-offy and vulgar. And there are adjectives that, when I first encountered them, moved me enough to clip them but have since, in my opinion, become clichés. These would include *vertiginous, lubricious, snarky, febrile, sclerotic, priapic, cloacal, etiolated, twee, soigné, pellucid, perfervid, palpable, lambent, plangent, iconic,* and *pneumatic* (as in "Renoir's pneumatic nudes").

With the help of modern computer databases, it's possible to look at this objectively. Consider *sclerotic* and *thrombotic*. Both originated as medical terms, the former referring to body or plant tissue that has thickened or hardened, the latter to the presence of artery-blocking blood clots. *Sclerotic* also has a metaphoric meaning, referring to people or organizations that have become rigid with age. This meaning has now officially lost any freshness or cleverness it once had. Keying in *sclerotic* to the LexisNexis databases of fifty major English-language newspapers, I see that the word has been employed 199 times in the past twelve months, almost always figuratively. This from the *Financial Times* is typical: "the UK economy combines many of the US economy's imbalances with productivity and demographic trends that look sclerotic even by European standards." And *thrombotic*? It was used twenty-five times—but twenty-four of them were in the medical sense. The single person who used it imaginatively was Dan Mitchell, referring in the *New York Times* to a time not long ago "when local news outlets were still flooding the zone every time a new Krispy Kreme store opened (but generally ignoring openings of the vastly superior, if equally thrombotic, Dunkin' Donuts)." Now that's a good adj.

Of course, there are different clichés for different fields. Reviewers of all kinds are probably the most notorious abusers and overusers of adjectives, plugging them into sentences and relieving themselves of the need to think. The condition was nailed by a recent *New Yorker* cartoon, in which a man looks up from a book and declares, "Forceful, yes! But not lucid, as the 'Times' would have me believe."

In his book *Passage to Juneau*, Jonathan Raban has a nice riff on how our perception of the world can actually be altered by clichéd adjectives:

Two centuries of romanticism, much of it routine and degenerate, has blunted everyone's ability to look at waterfalls and precipices in other than dusty and secondhand terms. Motoring through the Sound, watching for deadheads, I sailed through a logjam of dead literary clichés: snow-capped peaks above, fathomless depths below, and, in the middle of the picture, the usual gaunt cliffs, hoary crags, wild woods and crystal cascades.

Raban is himself an adjectival virtuoso, and I call your attention to the pair of paired adjectives in the first sentence of the passage: routine and degenerate, dusty and secondhand. Not only is it difficult to extract just the right doozy of an adjective out of the hornbook, but the maneuver can be performed at most twice in the course of an article or chapter. Any more than that and you look like a show-off. A more durable and ulti-mately more satisfying strategy is what Raban is doing here: using the conventional adjective in an unconven-tional way.

And so here is a selection of more or less familiar adjectives, used to splendid effect in unexpected ways:

"His passes were very specific." —Former basketball player Bobby Jones on his teammate Maurice Cheeks

"[T. S.] Eliot . . . would on occasion provide firm and worldly advice, even to unlikely and mutinous loners like Wyndham Lewis." —Donald Davie

"The government of the United States, in both its
legislative arm and its executive arm, is ignorant,
corrupt and disgusting." —H. L. Mencken

"Your old-fashioned tirade—/loving, rapid, merci-
less—/breaks like the Atlantic Ocean on my
head." —Robert Lowell

"[Andrew] Sarris's prose was dense, balanced, apho-
ristic, alliterative. . . . [Pauline] Kael's was loping,
derisive, intimate, gag-packed, as American as
Lenny Bruce." —Richard Corliss

"The American anti-Communism of the Fifties was
abstract, extreme, self-serving, and false." —John
Lukacs

"Society, in these States, is cankered, crude, super-
stitious, and rotten." —Walt Whitman

". . . the life of man, solitary, poor, nasty, brutish and
short." —Thomas Hobbes

"Housman is dry, soft, shy, prickly, smooth, conventional, silent, feminine, fussy, persnickety, sensi-
tive, tidy, greedy, and a touch of a toper."
—Harold Nicolson on A. E. Housman

You'll notice that there's a different feel depending
on whether one, two, three, or four or more adjectives
are used. In an ingenious article called "The Rhetoric of

the Series," the composition scholar Winston Weathers argued that by forming series of various lengths, writers present greatly different tones of voice. Two parts suggest "certainty, confidence, didacticism and dogmatism"; three parts, "the normal, the reasonable, the believable and the logical" (see *red, white, and blue*); and four or more parts, "the human, emotional, diffuse and inexplicable."

Martin Amis is another contemporary adjective virtuoso (and, I suspect, a fellow collector), and here's one sentence where, in describing a single, he uses a double and a five-spot: "The word 'Larkinesque' used to evoke the wistful, the provincial, the crepuscular, the sad, the unloved; now it evokes the scabrous and the supremacist."

Raban and Amis are British, and I would have to say that adjective use is a bit more highly developed across the pond than it is in the U.S. But there are some standout American practitioners. One of them is *New York Times* popular music critic Jon Pareles, whose use of adjectives in his concert reviews is resourceful, invigorating, and fine:

[Ted Hawkins's] voice was woolly and pensive.

[Thelonious Monk's] touch was blunt and unpretty, and his solos were droll and suspenseful.

. . . a groan that's jaded, long-suffering, cranky and shrewd. [On Walter Becker's voice.]

[Aretha Franklin's] voice was creamy, loving, humble, sassy and indomitable.

Frenetic and offhand, deranged and savvy, funny and brutal, crisp and wayward, the Pixies brought their calmly schizophrenic, firmly dislocated rock to the Ritz on Friday night.

Adjective difficulties often come when writers want to say "good" or "bad" in a forceful or stylish way, but haven't thought enough about which word to choose. Kenneth Tynan's Oxford tutor wrote on one of Tynan's papers: "Keep a strict eye on eulogistic & dyslogistic adjectives—They shd *diagnose* (not merely blame) & distinguish (not merely praise)." The tutor was C. S. Lewis, a smart chap.

There are more useful negative adjectives than positive ones; and some people deploy them with genius. George Orwell will often devote several paragraphs of relatively noncommittal description of something he clearly doesn't approve of. Only then comes the money shot, in the form of an adjective like *abhorrent, unspeakable*, or *disgusting*. Once I worked with a food critic named Janet Bukovinsky, and I have always treasured her description of a certain dish: "desiccated and nasty." Pop-lingo terms like *bogus*, *whack*, *lame*, *clueless*, and *random* still have a certain zing even though they're past their prime. I recently was privileged to be present when my daughter Elizabeth and her friends analyzed the subtle distinctions among *shady*, *sketchy*, *creepy*, and *skeevy*.

Praise is tougher, in large part because verbal inflation has taken its toll on *wonderful*, *great*, *fantastic*, *awesome*, *terrific*, *fabulous*, *incredible*, *remarkable*, and all the rest. As a result, the most effective kind of praise is often by understatement: having a certain kind of person say that something you've done is "decent" or "not bad" can put you on cloud nine for a week. With the exception of *cool*, which retains its effectiveness after well over half a century, slang words—*groovy*, *phat*, *radical*, *smokin'*—have a very brief life span in which they can be used to express sincere enthusiasm. Then they revert to irony or, at best, expressions of a sort of mild sardonic approval. The main rule seems to be, the simpler, the better. Robert Frost's most famous poem says, "The woods are lovely, dark and deep," and William Carlos Williams talks about plums that were "so sweet/and so cold." Huck Finn tells us, "I laid there in the grass and the cool shade thinking about things, and feeling rested and ruther comfortable and satis- fied"—and the four plain adjectives make us feel his pleasure.

Indeed, the most memorable literary adjective in the entire language is just four letters long. It appears in the fourth verse of the first book of the Bible: "And God saw the light, that it was good."

A GLOSSARY OF UNUSUAL ADJECTIVES

aleatoric: relating to luck, especially to bad luck.

alembicated: overrefined or oversubtle (said of ideas or expressions).

anfractuous: full of windings and intricate turnings.

anodyne: unlikely to offend or arouse tensions; innocuous.

baleful: threatening, or seeming to threaten, harm.

bibulous: marked by the consumption of alcoholic beverages.

bumptious: presumptuously, obtusely, and often noisily self-assertive.

capacious: containing or capable of containing a great deal.

captious: tending to find and stress faults and raise objections.

cartilaginous: composed of, relating to, or resembling
    cartilage.

cloacal: relating to, figuratively or literally, the common
    chamber into which the intestinal, urinary, and
    generative canals of many animals discharge; having
    to do with sewers or cesspools.

contumelious: insolently abusive and humiliating.

coprophagic: prone to, subject to, or characterized by the
    eating of excrement.

corybantic: wild; frenzied.

crepuscular: of, relating to, or resembling twilight.

cumbrous: cumbersome.

defunctive: having ceased to exist or live.

demotic: characteristic of ordinary people, especially in
    regard to language and speech.

dyslogistic: expressing or connoting disapprobation or
    dispraise.

etiolated: pale; lacking in natural vigor.

eulogistic: having the quality of high praise.

factitious: contrived or insincere.

febrile: feverish.

fissiparous: tending to break up into parts.

fustian: high-flown or affected in style.

gormless: stupid.

hieratic: highly stylized or formal.

hippoerotic: sexually stimulated by horses.

irrefrangible: impossible to refute, break, or alter.

lambent: marked by lightness or brilliance.

liminal: barely perceptible.

lubricious: marked by wantonness; salacious.

ludic: of, relating to, or characterized by play.

maledicent: reproachful (in speech); slanderous.

mephitic: foul-smelling.

mordant: biting and caustic in thought, manner, or style.

noisome: offensive to the senses and especially to the sense
        of smell; by extension, highly obnoxious or
        objectionable.

nugatory: of little or no consequence.

oneiric: of or relating to dreams.

otiose: useless; futile.

palpable: capable of being touched or felt; tangible.

panoptic: presenting a comprehensive or panoramic
        view.

pellucid: very clear and easy to understand.

penumbrous: shadowy or indistinct.

perdurable: very durable.

perfervid: marked by overwrought or exaggerated emotion;
        excessively fervent.

pertinacious: stubbornly unyielding or tenacious.

pharaonic: enormous in size or magnitude.

phatic: of or relating to speech used for social or
    emotive purposes rather than for communicating
    information.

piacular: requiring expiation; wicked or blameworthy.

plangent: having an expressive and especially plaintive
    quality.

polyphiloprogenitive: extremely prolific.

priapic: phallic; relating to or preoccupied with virility.

proleptic: anticipatory.

rebarbative: repellant; irritating.

refulgent: radiant or resplendent.

riparian: relating to or living or located on the bank of a
    river or lake.

scabrous: dealing with suggestive, indecent, or scandalous
    themes.

sedulous: diligent and perseverant.

sentient: responsive to or conscious of sense impressions.

shambolic: disorganized or confused.

snarky: sarcastically demeaning.

soigné: elegantly maintained or designed; sleek.

supercilious: patronizing and haughty.

supererogatory: performed to an unrequired or unnecessary
    extent.

supernal: superlatively good, as if originating in the
    heavens.

synovial: relating to, secreting, or being synovia (the clear
   viscous fluids that lubricate the lining of joints).

tenebrous: dark or murky.

tensile: relating to or involving tension.

vertiginous: causing dizziness, especially by being very high,
   literally or metaphorically.

CHAPTER II

Adv.

Every word, when a grammarian knows not what to make of it, he calls an adverb.
—*Servius, fourth century C.E.*

The adverb is like the adjective only more so. That is, it is disrespected so generally and so forcefully that numerous babies get thrown out with some admittedly skeevy bathwater. There is a long tradition of this. In the eighteenth century, John Horne Tooke called the adverb "the common sink and repository of all heterogeneous and unknown corruptions." H. L. Mencken referred to it as "at best the stepchild of grammar." More recently, Phil Phantom wrote in his book *The Guide to Writing Good Trash*: "Lazy, shiftless, slothful creatures without spines use simple verbs and then tack on an adverb to make sense. Because we are sentient beings with a brain, spinal cord, and opposing thumbs, we have the ability to seek out and find the precise verb that best describes the action."

Noted novelists have thrown down the gauntlet as well. Gabriel García Márquez has announced that his book *Chronicle of a Death Foretold* contains but a single adverb—and that he has completely banished the part of speech from subsequent works. Elmore Leonard not long ago posted on the Web a list of writing rules to live by. Number 4 is "Never use an adverb to modify the word 'said.' " Leonard continued: "To use an adverb this way (or almost any way) is a mortal sin. The writer is now exposing himself in earnest, using a word that distracts from and can interrupt the rhythm of the exchange. I have a character in one of my books tell how she used to write historical romances 'full of rape and adverbs.' " Good one. Toni Morrison observed, "I never say, 'She says softly.' If it's not already soft, I have to leave a lot of space around it so a reader can hear it's soft." And finally, Stephen King stated in his book *On Writing*:

I believe the road to hell is paved with adverbs, and I will shout it from the rooftops. To put it another way, they're like dandelions. If you have one on your lawn, it looks pretty and unique. If you fail to root it out, however, you find five the next day . . . fifty the day after that . . . and then, my brothers and sisters, your lawn is **totally, completely,** and **profligately**

covered with dandelions. By then you see them for
the weeds they are, but by then it's *GASP!!*—too
late.

Even Hollywood scriptwriters have joined in the
fun. In the thriller *Outbreak*, Kevin Spacey's character
picks on a word in a memo written by fellow scientist
Dustin Hoffman: "It's an adverb, Sam. It's a lazy tool of
a weak mind."

The flaw in all this calumny is exposed in a final
anti-adverb sound bite, this from the authors of a book
entitled *Self-Editing for Fiction Writers*, who advise: "Cut
virtually every one you write." A bright fourth-grader
would be delighted to tell them that in dissing adverbs,
they used an adverb. *Virtually*. And so did Phantom
(*best*), Leonard (*never*, *almost*), Morrison (*already*), and
King (*however*, *too*).

The root problem here is that the adverb is so varied
and various. It accounts for less than 5 percent of the
100-million-word British National Corpus and none of
the fifty most commonly used words in it (the top adverb is *so*, clocking in at number fifty-six), but David
Crystal, author of *The Cambridge Encyclopedia of the
English Language*, rightly calls it "the most heterogeneous of all the word classes in English grammar." The

adverb indeed can be a crutch and a peril, but it's also a tool necessary for expressing a multitude of meanings; and it can be an indispensable tool in crafting strong and artful prose.

You can get a sense of the adverb's potency by taking a glimpse at some titles that contain one. In each case the adverb rescues the title from blandness with a *je ne sais quoi* flavor:

- Movies: *Thoroughly Modern Millie*; *Truly Madly Deeply*; *Johnny Dangerously* (which contains the immortal line of dialogue: "Did you know your last name's an adverb?"); *And Now for Something Completely Different*.
- TV shows: *Absolutely Fabulous*; *Fairly Odd Parents*; *Suddenly Susan*; *A Very Brady Christmas*.
- Books: *Deeper into Movies*; *Bang the Drum Slowly*.
- Plays: *How to Succeed in Business Without Really Trying*; *Merrily We Roll Along*; *All's Well That Ends Well*.
- Songs: "Alone Again, Naturally"; "How High the Moon"; "Don't You Love Her Madly"; "This Was a Real Nice Clambake"; "Helplessly Hoping"; "Hopelessly Devoted to You"; and at least three from Bob Dylan: "Queen Jane Approximately,"

"Positively Fourth Street," and "Absolutely Sweet Marie."*

Adverbs can be bad; adverbs can be good. But how do you tell the difference? A good way to start is with an adverb taxonomy.

As recorded in the British National Corpus, the thirty most commonly used adverbs, after *so*, are *up, then, out, now, only, just, more, also, very, well, how, down, back, on, there, still, even, too, here, where, however, over, in, as, most, again, never, why, off*, and *really*. Unless you're a grammarian or I'm mistaken, you did a double-take when you read that list and muttered something along the lines of "Those aren't even adverbs, you twit!" But they are. It's true that only the last one, *really*, takes the traditional, well-known *adjective+ly* form, and it's true that some of these words do word-class double duty (*in, on*, and *over* can be prepositions, *as* a conjunction, *still* an adjective). But they are adverbs nonetheless. They modify adjectives, verbs, or both. She is *so* happy. He went *up*. *Then* I did it. We went *out*. Don't be *too* upset.

* The last mentioned contains a nice adverb-flavored couplet: "Well, anybody can be just like me, obviously / But then, now again, not too many can be like you, fortunately."

According to grammarians, adjectives, nouns, verbs, and interjections are considered "open" parts of speech, both because they can shift functions (e.g., *Pimp My Ride*) and because new words (e.g., *cyberspace*) are continually added to their ranks. Articles, conjunctions, prepositions, and pronouns are "closed" because, well, they're closed. Adverbs, uniquely, are mixed. I call the ones in the closed group—which include the first twenty-nine adverbs listed above—stealth adverbs. They are probably the most underrated subpart of speech and they are absolutely essential to communication. They're the mortar that holds our expressed thoughts together; you can't write a meaningful paragraph or have a meaningful conversation without them. They let language express relationship, context, causality, location, attitude, direction, and degree. Like Eskimos and their supposed multitude of snow terms, we have a lot of words indicating all these things, each one with a slightly different meaning or nuance from the other. Take a word like *even*, and think of the different shades of meaning it gives the base meaning of these sentences: "My boss gave me a raise and even told me I was doing a good job"; "My desk is even messier than his"; "Even Stephen King has writer's block sometimes." Our lives are such that we think a lot about how often things happen. Linguist Geoffrey Leech tabulated a list of frequency adverbs in order of frequency and, not surprisingly, the top five, accounting for more than two-thirds of all uses, were stealth adverbs. The top twenty: *never, always, often, ever, sometimes, usually, once, generally, hardly, no longer, normally, increasingly, twice, frequently, rarely, in general, occasionally, mostly, regularly,* and *constantly.*

The second half of that list is dominated by the adverb that gets the most ink and is certainly the easiest kind to spot. These are the words that are derived from the archaic form *adjective+like,* and now take the form *adjective+ly.* In the middle of the second millennium, as modern English was taking shape, there was a veritable frenzy of adverb creation using this formula, and Shakespeare alone coined a half dozen of them: *importantly, instinctively, obsequiously, threateningly, tightly,* and, most famously, the key word in Hamlet's speech to the players: "Speak the speech, I pray you, *trippingly* on the tongue."

The pattern is simple, but it has the potential to create some problems. *Friendly, deadly, lovely, unseemly, likely, comely,* and a recent addition I'm fond of, *studly,* are adjectives despite ending in *-ly.* You can make adverbs from them by turning the final *y* into an *i* and appending another *-ly,* but the resulting words are tough to pronounce and are rarely if ever spoken aloud. Still,

they can be found in the dictionary and are occasionally trotted out as a literary novelty item. From the first
line of Philip K. Dick's *Do Androids Dream of Electric
Sheep?*: "Friendlily, because he felt well-disposed toward
the world . . . he patted her bare, pale shoulder."

On the other hand, some adjectives do double duty
as adverbs and don't need the suffix. Former president
Bill Clinton once said, "The Bible defines a good life
thusly: 'To love justice, to do mercy, and to walk
humbly with thy God.' " With all due respect, *thusly* is
a non-word, as are *fastly*, *muchly*, *doubtlessly*, and *hardly*
(as in "He hit the ball *hardly*"). *Thus*, *fast*, *much*, *doubt-
less*, and *hard* work just fine as adverbs. *Finely* can indeed be an adverb (as in the way you might chop an
onion), but so is the *fine* in the previous sentence. It's
in the category that some grammarians refer to as "flat
adverbs." They were much more prevalent in centuries
past. Defoe refers in *Robinson Crusoe* to the weather being "so violent hot," and when Christopher Marlowe
wrote "Is it not *passing* brave to be a king?" he was taking the adverb *surpassingly* and subjecting it to both
shortening and flattening.

Nowadays, one often has a choice between an *-ly* adverb and a flattened form without it—as in such pairs as
bad and *badly*, *close* and *closely*, *bright* and *brightly*, *slow*
and *slowly*, *sure* and *surely*, *loud* and *loudly*, *deep* and

deeply, and *tight* and *tightly*. Writing tends to favor the former and speech the latter. The flattened adverb was a key to Mark Twain's formulation of the greatest colloquial voice in American literature. In the first chapter of *Adventures of Huckleberry Finn*, Huck tells us that the Widow Douglas "learned me about Moses and the Bulrushers, and I was in a sweat to find out all about him; but by and by she let it out that Moses had been dead a *considerable* long time; so then I didn't care no more about him, because I don't take no stock in dead people." James Brown sang, "I feel good [not *well*]," and, "Say it loud [not *loudly*], I'm black and I'm proud," and in her spoken intro to "Proud Mary," Tina Turner told us, "We never ever do nothing nice and *easy*—we always do it nice and *rough*." Sometimes the choice isn't so easy. Usage manuals and grammar books have been debating for more than two centuries the relative merits of and minute distinctions in meaning among "I feel *good*" and "I feel *well*," "I feel *bad*" and "I feel *badly*." The matter has not yet been resolved and does not look to be soon. In general the best course of action is to pay attention to context. Certainly, you would come off like a hopeless dweeb if you murmured to your beloved, "Hold me tightly. I want you so badly."

But there are relatively few acceptable flattened forms, in any case, compared to the multitude of *-ly* adverbs. These are common, familiar, and capable of seemingly endless variation: Dick ran swiftly. The river swiftly ran. Jane inexcusably rambled. Tom said eagerly . . .

. . . which brings me, inevitably, to the only (to my knowledge) genre of joke devoted to trashing a part of speech: the Tom Swifty. The name derives from the series of juvenile novels published beginning in 1894 and featuring the boy inventor Tom Swift. Edward L. Stratemeyer and his legion of ghostwriters never allowed Tom merely to "say" anything. Instead, they penned lines like these (from actual Tom Swift books):

" 'Hello, Ned Newton!' called Tom, heartily."

Or:

"Tom tore open the envelope, and rapidly scanned the contents of the missive. 'Hello!' he ejaculated half aloud."

In February 1963, a lighthearted time, an anonymous writer at *Playboy* magazine invented a new type of pun: a fabricated Tom Swift–like line of dialogue in which the adverb modifying *said* humorously refers to or plays on the subject of the quote. Examples would include: " 'I can no longer hear anything,' Tom said deftly." " 'I need a pencil sharpener,' Tom said bluntly." " 'I only have diamonds, clubs, and spades,'

Tom said heartlessly." Since then the Tom Swifty has trudged on, not exactly swiftly but with an impressive staying power. You can find Web sites that list as many as nine hundred of them. As the above examples suggest, Tom Swifties are virtually never funny,* but they illustrate an adverb-centered sin against writing. You can sum it up in the time-honored phrase: show, don't tell. Adverbs, especially -ly adverbs, are fatally prone to "telling." As Phil Phantom (love that name) suggests, quite often the decision to stick an adverb in is at once a sign of laziness and of protesting too much. The writer hasn't bothered to find just the right verb, and so inserts the adverb the way a defendant throws

---

* Indeed, they are usually so profoundly unfunny that when I read them my face forms an involuntary frown. They have a mechanical quality, and in fact a team of linguists wrote a program that allows computers to construct Tom Swifties. The results are no less funny than those composed by humans, but no funnier, either. Speaking of the academic study of Tom Swifties, an experiment by psychologist Louis G. Lippman bears out my opinion of them. Lippman showed Tom Swifties to research subjects and asked them to rate how humorous the japes were on a scale of 1 (not at all) to 5 (extremely). The mean rating was 2.4, and was probably that high because of the politeness factor. Having read hundreds of Tom Swifties, I have come across only two that I consider even moderately funny. " 'I manufacture tabletops for shops,' said Tom counterproductively." And: " 'I'm not sure I'm a homosexual,' said Tom, half in Ernest."

himself on the mercy of the court. It doesn't take all that much time or effort to come up with *he shouted* as a replacement for *he said loudly*, or *she sprinted* as a fix for *she ran quickly*. In cases like these, the substitution makes for cleaner, more precise, and more forceful prose.

On the other hand, sometimes you need to use one of these adverbs. That's because there just aren't that damned many verbs. Certainly, none exists that could adverblessly express the meaning of "he stirred the pot *slowly*" or "she *carefully* dressed the baby" or "he waxed the car *meticulously*." Sure, you could convey the idea in the last example by saying something like "He spent forty minutes waxing the car. Each time he finished a spot he stared at it with his brow furrowed, as if he were convinced that a flaw simply had to be there." But that takes more time and space than most of us have at our disposal.

People with complicated things to say, many of them describing or remarking on subtle relationships, impressions, or gradations, use adverbs to get the idea across. Here is the first paragraph of Martin Amis's review of Tom Wolfe's novel *A Man in Full*, with the adverbs in boldface:

This book will be a good friend to you. Maybe the best you **ever** had—or so it will **sometimes** seem. I read *A Man in Full* during a week of lone travel, and it was **always** there for me: nestling in my lap on planes and trains, enlivening many a solitary meal, and **faithfully** waiting in my hotel room when I returned, last thing. Like its predecessor, *The Bonfire of the Vanities*, Tom Wolfe's new novel is **fiercely** and **instantly** addictive. It is **intrinsically** and **generically** disappointing, too, bringing with it an unavoidable hangover. But a **generously** mild one, **really**, considering the time you had.

Adverbially, a number of things stand out about the passage. First, adverbs constitute 9.4 percent of the total words—a substantially higher percentage than the norm. The ones in the beginning are the stealth adverbs, those simple modifiers that anonymously give a sentence specificity and precision—*ever, sometimes, always*. As Amis warms to his theme, he deploys the showier *-ly* adverbs, in rapid-fire succession, and they allow him to fine-tune his judgments. The final five all modify adjectives rather than verbs, which I find significant. Adjectives and adverbs alike, alone, are prone to tell-don't-show. But pairing them yields synergy. Amis describes *A Man in Full* as *fiercely and instantly addictive*. By itself *addictive* would have been a cliché, but the adverbs take the sting out; they buff up a tired epithet by giving it a rate of speed and human (or animal) characteristics.

Adverbs and adjectives tend to work best together when they're previously unacquainted and cut against each other's grain in a salutary way. In "Desolation Row," Bob Dylan tells us about "Einstein, disguised as Robin Hood": he "looked so *immaculately frightful* as he bummed a cigarette." A later singer-songwriter, Phil Roy, has a great song called "Undeniably Human." Novelist Will Self once referred to a character taking a file from "a briefcase of *achingly sensible* utility." Gerald Nachman called his book on the comedians of the 1950s and '60s *Seriously Funny*, and Steven Levy called *his* book on the Macintosh computer *Insanely Great*. In an essay in *The Writer* magazine, Arthur Plotnik went so far as to suggest a formula: "Take a forceful adjective (say 'withering'), add '-ly' to make it an adverb, combine it with the target word (say, 'cute'), and voilà— 'witheringly cute,' a burst of wry wit, a mini-statement."

Having touched on the adverb's potential for glory, or at least eloquence, let me return to the dark side and begin with qualifiers. These are the weaselly terms like *somewhat, comparatively, relatively, essentially, nearly, almost, fairly, slightly, more or less, kind of, sort of, rather, a bit, basically,* and five expressions that, in 1942, Harold Ross banished from *The New Yorker*'s pages: *pretty, oddly enough*, *vaguely*, *faintly*, and *a little*. (In the same directive, Ross also banned the adverb *wistfully*.) Related is the overuse of understatement, as in the rhetorical form known as litotes, for example, "I was not unhappy to be there." A little of this goes a long way. George Orwell counseled, "One can cure oneself of the *not un-* formation by memorizing this sentence: *A not unblack dog was chasing a not unsmall dog across a not ungreen field.*" In all cases, the problem is clear. People qualify when they haven't decided what they want to say, or have decided but don't have the courage to stand behind it, or simply feel the need to clear their throat in the middle of a sentence. Fowler blamed qualifier-mania on "the notion that a studious air of understatement is superior and impressive" and cast as the villain of the piece the newspapers, where "the intemperate orgy of moderation is renewed every morning."

Two qualifiers deserve special mention. In recent years, journalists have gone on an *arguably* spree, in such sentences as "Donovan McNabb is arguably the best quarterback in the National Football League." What does that mean? That the writer thinks McNabb is the best quarterback in the National Football League (TBQITNFL)? That some (conveniently unnamed) people have made an argument that he is TBQITNFL? Or merely that the writer is too lazy to form an opinion and support the position that McNabb is TBQITNFL and hides behind a bogus adverb? My money's on number three.

Then there's a word familiar to every parent of a teenager—*like*, as in the sentences "I want to like go to law school," "He's like twenty," or, most notoriously, "I was like, 'You have got to be kidding me!' " This use of *like*—to somehow like (sorry) vaguely undermine or fuzz up what comes after it—appears to have had its origin in the beatnik era. Certainly the first well-known figure to utilize it was the character Maynard G. Krebs on TV's *The Many Loves of Dobie Gillis*, whose trademark catchphrase was "Like wow, Dobe." It was dormant for a couple of decades, then revived by Moon Unit Zappa's 1982 song "Valley Girl," which contained the immortal line "He was like so gross." The usage has been around ever since and shows no sign of abating. The standard view of this *like* is as a vogue-word space filler, like *um* or *you know*, only more insidious and infuriating. But I like *like*. Uttered in an appropriate context by a person of an appropriate age, *like* conveys a sense of approximation and equivocation, both of which are often useful to teens. "I want to go to law school" would be too definitive, certain, almost strident. The *like* takes the edge off. The word can also save you from sounding pompous. A twenty-four-year-old woman was quoted in the *New York Times* criticizing the city's plan to inspect subway riders' bags: "It's a complete obstruction of, like, freedom."

Nor does *like*'s use, combined with *to be*, as a verb of attribution deserve the scorn heaped on it. The alternative to "I was like, 'You have got to be kidding me!' " is "I said, 'You have got to be kidding me!' " Besides being unduly formal, the second version indicates that the words inside the single quotes were the exact ones spoken. However, the point of such a statement would probably be to give not an exact transcription but a general sense of the comment, and *I was like* gives this idea. (The similar term *all*, as in "I was all, 'You have got to be kidding me!' " is even more approximate.)

A converse to the qualifier problem is the overuse, or even the use, of intensifiers, sometimes known as amplifiers: *certainly, really, quite, definitely, totally, completely, absolutely, extremely, awfully, incredibly, unbelievably, clearly*, and the like. The sheer number of them, all with more or less the same meaning, is significant. If you haven't made your case, you have to pound the adverbial drums, the same way the boy in the story had to insist that this time, there really, really, *really* was a wolf. In fact, *really*'s pretty much only legitimate function occurs in imitations of Katharine Hepburn, Ed Sullivan, and Elmer Fudd (respectively, "Raally, I do";

"really big shew"; and "weawwy wascawwy wabbit"). The word is so desperately overused that it makes statements less convincing, not more. The following post to a British computer bulletin board devoted to rap music really doesn't make me want to go out and buy the CD under discussion:

> I'm also really into The Streets, just now and again—I really like their second album, A Grand Don't Come For Free. The whole album has got an underlying story all the way through. As you listen to each track, you get a bit more of the story. Really clever. You do have to REALLY listen to it though!

The Longman Grammar of Written and Spoken English lists the frequency of the most common intensifiers in three different idioms. British English conversation: *very, so, really, too, absolutely, bloody, real, completely, totally,* and *damn.* American English conversation: *so, very, really, too, real* (a flat adverb, as in "I'm real hungry"), *totally, completely, absolutely,* and *damn.* Academic prose: *very, so, too, extremely, highly, entirely, fully,* and *completely.*

Very's very popularity (and brevity) makes it the most insidious intensifier. I once had the bracing experience of receiving back a copyedited book manuscript of mine in which every one of my fourscore uses of the word had been deleted. Much as I tried, I could muster no defense for three quarters of them, and they stayed gone, to the betterment of the book. Johnny Mercer, sensing that the only possible way to use this word in a song lyric was to divorce it from an adjective and double it up, put this lovely couplet in "Too Marvelous for Words": "You're much too much, and just too very very/To ever be in Webster's Dictionary." (And anyone who rigidly rejects the splitting of infinitives should meditate on the profound lameness of "ever to be in Webster's Dictionary.")

As for *so*, it has a long and instructive backstory. As the Old English word *swa* it was an adverb indicating something done in a specified manner or degree or as a result of a specified reason or to a specified extent, the way we would still say, "He did so yesterday," or "If you're going, so will I," or "There's no food, so we'll have to go to the market." It was a small step to place the word before an adjective, follow it with a *that*, and use it in a comparative sense, almost as an equivalent to *sufficiently*, as Henry Fielding did in his novel *Tom Jones*: "The Squire was so delighted with this conduct of his daughter, that he scarce eat any dinner." The next step removed that *that*, letting *so* stand alone as an intensifier. Henry Richardson used it this way in another eighteenth-century novel, *Pamela*: "My face . . . was hid in my bosom, and I looked so silly!" The usage ambled happily along for a lengthy period, until the late twentieth century, when youth slang hijacked *so* and messed with its DNA. For the first time, people (both in real life and on *Friends*) followed it with *negative* adjectives or adjective phrases ("That's so not funny" [compare the traditional "That's not so funny"—almost the same thing, but not quite]), or with nouns or noun phrases (as in "That's so you" or "That's so ten minutes ago" or the kids' TV program *That's So Raven*). This usage was clever for a while but like most wacky fads could stay viable only with increasingly rococo variations, like "I'm so not going." The inevitable verdict now is that it's so over.

So is used as an adverb in a remarkable number of other ways, confirming the axiom that the smallest words have the most varied and complicated meanings. It can be used to mean something like *therefore* or *as a result*, as in "It's raining, so we'll drive," or *indeed* in an answer to an accusation of negligence ("I did so!"), and it has varying meanings in *and so on*, *so be it*, *so much for* . . . , *so there*, and *so what?* As the opening word of a sentence, it gives the idea of *it appears that* or *I gather that* ("So we meet at last!"), or—reflecting Yiddish idiom—*well then*, *in that case*, *very well*, or *anyway*, as in the exchange of dialogue the *OED* quotes from an Ed

McBain novel: " 'I warn you . . . I ain't got no wine.' 'So who wants wine?' " Seamus Heaney's translation of the Anglo-Saxon epic *Beowulf* audaciously begins: "So. The Spear-Danes in days gone by and the kings who ruled them had courage and greatness." I've always felt this usage carried with it a faint sense of challenge or even threat, and it seemed odd that a popular series of children's books in my youth would carry titles like *So You Want to Be an Astronaut.* I see that Amazon carries 793 books that begin with the words *So You Want to Be . . .* The bestselling title at the moment is *So, You Want to Be Like Christ?* (The books are about evenly divided on the interesting question-mark question. With the *?* the title has that confrontational sound, and without it is an evenhanded observation.) The Yiddish word *nu*, uttered alone with a rising intonation, means "So?" As in "Sue Me," a song from *Guys and Dolls*, it's often used with pleonastic (that is, intentional) redundancy: "So *nu?*"

As all this may suggest, the value of intensifiers is in nonstandard usage. You could date and place a hipster with some precision by whether he or she dressed up adjectives and verbs with *wicked* (New England's favorite), *steady* (which indicates in the African-American vernacular that an action is "intense, consistent and continuous," in the words of one scholar), *way* (as in

Wayne's World–style *way cool*), *hella*, *stone*, *cold* ("he cold dissed the guy"), *straight* ("that dress is straight ugly"), *uber*, *super*, *scary*, or *mad*. Jewish hipsters are fond of the extremely useful Yiddish word *tahkeh*. None of the above takes the *adjective+ly* form, and slang intensifiers rarely do, probably because it comes off a bit bourgeois and straitlaced. (The one exception I can think of is the piquant *majorly*.)

Off-color words have estimable intensifying power. These begin with the unholy trinity of *damned* (or *damn*, or *goddamn/ed*), *bloody*, and *fucking* and all their substitutes and euphemistic attendants: respectively, *darned*, *danged*, and *deuced*; *bleeding* and *blooming*; and *flipping*, *frigging*, *fricking*, *effing*, *bleeping* (derived ono-matopoetically from the electronic sound broadcasters use to cover unacceptable words), and the little-used but effective *schmucking*. (From the Internet: "Why the schmucking idea of presenting another Birth Cert to prove that we're the same person standing in front of the counter?") Oddly, these words intensify in opposite directions depending on whether they're used as adjectives or adverbs. In the former case, they usually have a negative connotation ("You're a *damned* liar"), in the latter a positive or at least appreciative one ("This drink is *effing* strong"). In a classic 1980 article in the journal *American Speech*, James B. McMillan coined the term "infixing" to describe cases where the expletive or euphemism is inserted into a word so as to intensify its force: for example, *abso-blooming-lutely* (used in the song "Wouldn't It Be Loverly?" in *My Fair Lady*) or *un-fucking-believable*. McMillan notes that infixing commonly occurs within polysyllabic words but sometimes also in the middle of phrases (as in "the United bloody Kingdom"—Graham Greene, *The Honorary Consul*) and, to his knowledge, once in the middle of a one-syllable word. This came from an informant who reported a drill sergeant's trademark command: *Mar-fucking-ch*. The contemporary master of infixing is, of course, Ned Flanders on *The Simpsons*, who inserts his very own infix—*diddily*—whenever possible. In moments of stress or frustration, Flanders's infixing seems to possess him, as in the episode when he said: "I just can't dang diddily do dang do damn diddily darn do it."

Most grammar books agree that some adverbs can modify whole sentences. Unsurprisingly, grammarians refer to these words as "sentence adverbs." *Unsurprisingly*, as I just used it, is such an adverb. It describes not the way grammarians speak, but rather the whole idea that is about to be expressed. Certain sentence adverbs refer to the speaker or writer's attitude, so that a sentence beginning with *adjective+ly* means "I am being [*adjective*] when I tell you that . . ." Examples include *confidentially*, *briefly*, *seriously*, *truthfully*, and Rhett Butler's "Frankly, my dear, I don't give a damn." An impressive number of sentence adverbs are in frequent current use, including *clearly*, *strangely*, *indeed*, *theoretically*, *naturally*, *conceivably*, *seriously*, *ultimately*, *therefore*, *basically*, *surprisingly*, *ironically*, *predictably*, *fortunately*, *however*, and *incidentally*. (Fowler says of the last: "Those who find it most useful are not the best writers.") One thinks of a few of these words—*evidently*, *apparently*, *supposedly*, *presumably*—as being favorites of the postwar educated class. Certainly, the dialogue in John Updike's fiction is peppered with them.

The sentence adverbs are an odd group. They are of undeniable assistance in conveying one's attitude, but there is something a little shifty about them. The brilliant writers of the sitcom *Seinfeld* nailed this in a scene that has made me unable, probably forever, to take a certain sentence adverb seriously. The hapless character George has come to retrieve his car from a parking lot, and finds not only that it has been used by prostitutes for assignations, but that it has been blocked by other cars and won't be available for a couple of days. The attendant, speaking in one of the indeterminate foreign accents *Seinfeld* was so fond of, says, "We ask that you please bear with us."

GEORGE: Bear with you! This is a parking lot. PEOPLE
ARE SUPPOSED TO BE ABLE TO GET THEIR CARS!!!
ATTENDANT: Ideally.*

A long-standing grammatical shibboleth holds that
in a sentence such as "More importantly, they won
the game," one should replace the sentence adverb
with *important*, on the grounds that what the speaker
really means is "What is more important, they won the
game." *Merriam-Webster's Guide to English Usage* (in common with other sensible guides) grants permission to use
either formulation: "both are defensible grammatically,
and both are in respectable use." The book similarly
okays the use of *firstly* and *secondly* as sentence adverbs, as
well as Miss Grundy's preferred *first* and *second*.

The single most abused and annoying sentence adverb is
actually. The word has a respectable pedigree and a legitimate meaning; inserted in a sentence, it stresses the real-

* Predictably, a Web site exists that contains a searchable archive
of every word uttered in a *Seinfeld* episode. I keyed in "ideally"
and found the exchange above, and one other, equally devastating. George and Jerry are at the coffee shop and George is regret-
ting having told a woman he loves her, because "Nobody wants
to be with somebody that loves them."
JERRY: No, people hate that.
GEORGE: You want to be with somebody that doesn't like you.
JERRY: Ideally.

ity or factuality of what is being stated. In *Pride and Prejudice*, Jane Austen has a character say, "As I have actually paid the visit, we cannot escape the acquaintance now." It can also be used to indicate surprise. At a recent meeting of the English department at the school where I teach, a memo written by me was discussed. I was not pleased to observe no fewer than three colleagues stand up and utter some variation of "I think Ben may actually be right." The degeneration of *actually* is signaled by a Doonesbury cartoon in which a Hollywood mogul, Mr. Kibbitz, instructs his young associate: "Listen, Jason, if you're going to make it in this town, you have to start using the word 'actually.' A Hollywood assistant *always* says, 'Actually, he's in a meeting,' or 'He's actually at lunch.' 'Actually' means 'I'm not lying to you.' "

The word at least has a denotative function in Kibbitz's analysis. But for some time, people have been overusing *actually* to mean, well, nothing. My daughters watch a reality show called *America's Next Top Model*, which *should* be called *Actually America's Next Top Model*, so often is the word thrown around. In one episode I happened to catch, the contestants were asked to perform mock interviews of one another. One pair perpetrated so many *actuallys* that a graphic on the bottom of the screen gave a running count. The total was eight times in fifteen seconds. None was actually necessary.

It would probably not be possible to write about sentence adverbs, or even to write about adverbs, or even to write about language, without the obligatory discussion of *hopefully*. So here it is, streamlined:

- As a sentence adverb meaning *I hope that*, one *hopes that*, or *it is to be hoped that* (as opposed to an older and universally accepted meaning, of doing something in a hopeful manner), *hopefully* has been in use since 1702, when it appeared in a book by Cotton Mather.
- It was used very rarely, however, until around 1960, when it became a vogue word. Immediately after that, it began to be decried, notably by Wilson Follett and in short order by Edwin Newman, Jacques Barzun, and John Simon. In fact, for a couple of decades, it appeared that a *hopefully* screed was the primary requirement for a language commentator to make his or her bones.
- The objections raised were various. Some were simply wrong—e.g., that an adverb couldn't modify a sentence. Others were debatable at best—e.g., that the sentence adverb would ruin *hopefully* in its traditional sense.
- After about a quarter century of sturm und

drang, a fairly sizable majority opinion
holds that, in the words of the 2003
Garner's Modern American Usage, "the battle is
now over. *Hopefully* is a part of [American
English]."

- Nevertheless, I still don't like the word. One
problem is it lacks etymological logic. *Sadly* means
"It is sad that . . ." *Frankly* means "I am being frank
when I say that . . ." *Predictably* means, "It was
predictable that . . ." *Hopefully* means "I hope
that . . ." and there is just no explaining away that
pesky *-ful*. The classic article critiquing the
criticisms of *hopefully* is M. Stanley Whitley's
"Hopefully: A Shibboleth in the English Adverb
System," which appeared in *American Speech* in
1983 and holds that attacks on the word boil down
to know-nothing snobbery. Whitley provided a list
of dozens of sentence adverbs, but not a single one
followed the same form as *hopefully*. *Truthfully*
(meaning "I am being truthful when I say that . . .")
is slightly related, and *thankfully* is quite close.
(*Thankfully* = "I am thankful that . . ."; *Hopefully* =
"I am hopeful that . . .") But neither word can be
taken as a historical precedent. The *OED*'s first
citation for *thankfully* as a sentence adverb is from

1966, and it doesn't list *truthfully* as a sentence
adverb at all, indicating an even more recent origin.*

• *Hopefully* is a useful term in conversation. If
someone asks you "When will the package get
there?," saying "Tomorrow, I hope" sounds a little
Pollyanna-ish and saying "Tomorrow, if all goes
well and the United States Postal Service lives
up to its reputation for promptness" is hopelessly
wordy. So "Tomorrow, hopefully" fills a need. But
I don't use *hopefully* in writing and I cast a cold
eye on those who do. Hoping is a vague,
unsophisticated, and largely uninteresting state
of mind. One associates it with children and
their feelings about birthday presents and snow
days. Compared to the surgical precision of
sentence adverbs like *presumably*, *ostensibly*, and
understandably, *hopefully* is a bowl of mush.

There is one more thing to say about adverbs. I have
saved it for last so you can skip it. I give you a chance
to skip it because it can drive you crazy.

---

* Things would be a lot easier if there were such a word as
hopable. That way, *hopefully* and *hopably* could follow the forms of
regretfully and *regrettably*: the first would refer to the state of mind
and the second to the situation.

The topic is location of adverbs in sentences. In many cases this is simple. When an adverb modifies an adjective, it almost always comes first: *very pretty, hopelessly devoted.** Adverbs can come before or after verbs depending on which word is meant to be emphasized. *He swam slowly* means something slightly different from *he slowly swam*. Things begin to get a little trickier when there is a direct object: one could use the structure "He warmly greeted the visiting relatives" or "He greeted the visiting relatives warmly" depending on which worked best in a particular sentence. Then there are cases when the verb includes an auxiliary or "helping" verb such as *be, have,* or *do,* or when it's in the infinitive form. Generations of grammar-school grammar teachers held that adverbs should never be insinuated into these verbs, so that instead of "should never be" I would have had to write "never should be." In the same way, you would have to perpetrate a sentence like "I saw Bill as he slowly was walking up the path" instead of the more natural "as he was slowly walking."

There's no good reason not to say it the natural way; the prohibition derives from the structure of Latin and has no business in English. A special and notorious case

* An exception might be a sentence like "She was pretty—beautiful, *even.*"

is the split infinitive: the idea—also derived from Latin, in which infinitive verbs are in the form of one word, not two—that you have to say, "I want you carefully to examine the article" instead of "to carefully examine." This has no justification, either, as sensible authorities have consistently pointed out for well over a hundred years. George Bernard Shaw called the prohibition "fatuous" and Ernest Gowers said it was "a bad rule"; even a stickler like Fowler referred to "the non-split diehard—bogy-haunted creatures . . . who would sooner be caught putting knives in their mouths as splitting an infinitive."

The thing that can drive you crazy is the placement of stealth adverbs like *just, even,* and, especially, *only.* The pioneering language maven Theodore Bernstein quoted a grammar guide that noted, "Eight different meanings result from placing 'only' in eight possible positions in the sentence: 'I hit him in his eye yesterday.'" (I'll pause while you work this out. My only quibble is that I can't quite see the difference between "I hit him only in his eye" and "I hit him in only his eye.") To understand precisely how this presents a problem, consider two sentences: a) "I only answered one question on the test." b) "I answered only one question on the test." The literal meaning of A is that the speaker only *answered* a question, as opposed to crossing it out, or coloring it in, or doing anything else to it. The literal meaning of B is that the speaker answered precisely *one* question, no more and no less. People almost always use A when they mean B. In today's paper, the golfer Vijay Singh is quoted as saying, "A playoff is match play. You only think one shot at a time." We understand that he means, "You think only one shot at a time." His order is the way people talk and write song titles. If it weren't, we would have the Beach Boys' "Only God Knows (What I'd Be Without You)" and the Ink Spots' "You Hurt Only the One You Love."

For a long time, it was the way I wrote. That all changed when the umpteenth copyeditor—it may have been the same one who took out all those *verys*—moved around an *only* in a sentence of mine. I was cured—but the side effect was that I started to see misplaced *onlys* everywhere I looked. As noted, they are the idiomatic standard in speech, but they've become pretty darned ubiquitous in print as well. I found the following in *The New Yorker*, long considered the pinnacle of American usage: "The Hutu didn't just kill the Tutsi, he points out. The Hutu also killed other Hutu." (*Just* operates here as a synonym for *only*.) My curse is that every time I read or hear a sentence of this type, I silently correct it—in this case, to "The Hutu didn't kill just the Tutsi . . ."

As is often the case, Fowler offers sage counsel on this issue: "For *he only died a week ago* no better defence is perhaps possible than that it is always the order that most people have always used and still use, and that, the risk of misunderstanding being chimerical, it is not worth while to depart from the natural."

Sage counsel it may be: but I sorrowfully predict that if you followed me this far, you too will be silently shuffling around *only*s for the rest of your days.

CHAPTER III

Art. Conj. Int. N. Prep. Pron. V. Adj. Adv.

A case can be made for the poet giving some of his life to the use of the words *the* and *a*: both of which are weighted with as much epos and historical destiny as one man can perhaps resolve.

—Louis Zukofsky

The definite and indefinite article, a.k.a. *the* and the duo of *a* and *an*, field the smallest roster of any part of speech but the biggest per-word punch. *The* is the most commonly used word in the English language, occurring nearly sixty-two thousand times in every million words written or uttered—or about once in every sixteen words. That's more than twice as often as the runner-up, *of*. A, meanwhile, places fifth and *an* comes in at thirty-fourth. (Third and fourth place go to *and* and *to*—not surprising since I just used them two times each in the space of four words.)*

---

* If it strikes you that the common words are all really short, you're on to something. The fifty-four most frequently used

It's readily apparent why we use *the* and *a* so often—
we need to identify and specify all those nouns that
populate the inner and outer universes. Nevertheless,
the early English grammarians did not recognize them
as constituting a separate part of speech, and opinion
was divided through the 1700s. "The fate of this very
necessary word has been most singularly hard and unfortunate," John Horne Tooke wrote at the end of the
century, referring to *the*. "For though without it, or
some equivalent invention, men could not communicate their thoughts at all; yet (like many of the most
useful things in this world) from its unaffected simplicity and want of brilliancy, it has been ungratefully ne-
glected and degraded." In recent years, grammarians
have tended to lump *the* and *a*—along with demonstratives (*that*, *this*, *these*, and *those*), possessives (*my*, *your*,
our, etc.), and quantifiers (*each*, *no*, *any*, *some*, *one*, *two*,
etc.)—in a word class known as "determiners." But I am
going to stick to articles, a category that, as Tooke recognized, has an estimable power. These two and a half
words are so ubiquitous, so rich and so odd, that they

---

words are all one syllable; then comes *about*. The most common
three-, four-, five-, and six-syllable words, with their overall
rankings in parentheses, are *government* (140), *information* (219),
international (415), and *responsibility* (1,102).

will take up my allotted space in this chapter and then some.

One peculiar thing about them is the variance they allow in pronunciation. Generally, we say "thee" instead of "thuh" when we pause or struggle for a word, for emphasis ("I met Lance Armstrong yesterday." "*Thee* Lance Armstrong?"), and, most commonly, when the following word begins with a vowel. But there are more exceptions to the last rule than you might expect. One study found that while 100 percent of people over fifty years old said *thee* before vowel-starting words, the rate for subjects in their twenties was only 63 percent. Furthermore, only half of New Yorkers followed the *thee*-vowel rule, compared to more than 80 percent of those from New England and the West. So a young guy from Queens is more likely than a middle-aged gent from Spokane to say something like "Yuh wanna go tuh thuh Eagles concuht tuhmarruh?"

A has two pronunciations as well, but neither I nor my team of crack research assistants has been able to find any scholarship on the question of when people say *ay* and when they say *uh*. My sense is that it's always *uh* except when speakers want to stress the word: "He is *a* [as opposed to *the*] vice president," or "I want *a* pancake," as opposed to three or four of them.

Everybody knows the general rule for when one uses

a or *an*, but there are some fine points and variations. According to a Web site devoted to Scots, it is permissible in that language to use *a* before a vowel; the example given is "Ah'll hae fower butteries, a crumpet an a aipple tairt." And abbreviations take indefinite articles according to how they sound, not how they're spelled: so it's "an NBA game" and "a UN mission." According to *Garner's Modern American Usage*, up until the nineteenth century, *an* was used before all words that started with a vowel, regardless of sound; the Constitution refers to "an uniform Rule of Naturalization." That sounds funny to our ears, as does the custom, still found in Britain and the most pretentious American circles, of using *an* before aspirated *h*'s, as in "an historic" and "an hero." As Mark Twain observed way back in 1882, "Correct writers of the American language do not put an *an* before those words." (On the other hand, we still say "an hour" because the *h* is silent.) I believe human history has witnessed only one example of the intentionally comical misuse of *an*. This was a *Saturday Night Live* skit in which one member of a stuck-up preppy family expressed her bemused terror at the ethnicity of a dinner guest by exclaiming: "Oh, an Puerto Rican!"

As for meaning, the differences between using *a* and *the* and omitting the article altogether (which linguists call the "zero article"; for indefinite plural or collective nouns one can use either the zero article or the word *some*) are so manifold and complicated that most grammar books take a pass on going into them and take the easy way out. That is, they say something to the effect that by the age of four, native English speakers know in their bones the difference between "I drank Coke," "I drank the Coke," and "I drank a Coke," and the fact that you take *a* pass but *the* easy way out. But someone trying to learn English as a second language, they go on to say, will never really master the intricacies, and so it's a waste of everyone's time to go into them. Those interested in the intricacies can, however, consult Huddleston and Pullum's comprehensive *Cambridge Grammar of the English Language*, which devotes five and a half closely argued pages to *a* and *the*, featuring such sentences as: "It is important to note, however, that the concept of totality implied by the definite article is somewhat weaker than that expressed by universal quantification: if the set consists of a number of essentially similar entities, then the use of the definite article does not entail that every individual entity has the predication property." (This means, essentially, that when you say, "The bathroom tiles are cracked," you don't necessarily mean to assert that every single tile is cracked.)

As this suggests, articles are a hard thing for people

studying English to master—maybe the hardest. The problem varies depending on the treatment of articles in one's native tongue. Romanian, Macedonian, Swedish, and Aztec append the definite article to the back of a noun, and Arabic to the front. (The man we know as Alexander the Great was born Iskander, a common Muslim name. "Al-Iskander" gives him the honorific *the*.) Swahili and Latin rarely use articles of any kind; author Charles Williams once speculated that the inability of Latin speakers to distinguish between *a* and *the* may have hastened the conception of the devil. Polish, Russian, and Japanese are article-less as well. Arabic, Welsh, and Esperanto have definite articles but no indefinite articles. In French and German, the definite article is applied to proper nouns and the names of abstractions and classes of things, so that a Parisian who hasn't completely mastered idiomatic English and who means to express that he fancies all solid savory dairy products, not merely a particular variety, will say something like "Me, I like the cheese." It's fortunate that no one grows up speaking Old English nowadays because such a person would go nuts trying to learn the modern variety: in the old form, *the* could be masculine, feminine, or neuter and had five case forms as a singular and four as a plural.

As noted in the introduction to this book, Harold Ross of *The New Yorker* despised *the* because of its capacity for indirection. Ross may have taken things too far, but four decades after his death, his suspicions about the sneakiness of the word received scientific confirmation. In 1992, in Amsterdam, a plane crashed into an apartment building. No film or video of the incident was taken. A couple of years later, researchers conducted a study in which subjects were asked: "Did you see *the* television film of *the* moment *the* plane hit *the* apartment building?" (italics added). Such was the power of multiple definite articles that 55 percent answered "Yes."

The *the* of broadcast news is *that*. Twenty years ago, a friend of mine named Chris, then a writer for a local TV news operation, told me that he and his colleagues were not permitted to compose such formulations as "*that* rowhouse fire," "*that* fast-approaching cold front," and "*that* flu epidemic." The objection (similar to Ross's gripe about *the*) was that the word was a cheesy and unearned way to imply familiarity. When I asked Chris about this a couple of weeks ago, he didn't remember the ban but directed me to the producer he worked under at the time. This man confirmed that he had indeed outlawed *that*, as well as such other pieces of journalese as *blaze* (for fire) and *probe* (for investigation). One thing Chris did recall was that at his next TV news job, he was actually commanded to use *that*, in order to communicate "that the story is something that viewer and reporter have been 'chatting' about on an ongoing basis."

I had a conversation with a British colleague not long ago in which she complained about *the* for a completely different reason—to her, it was an annoying Americanism. The particular thing that had gotten her going was Yanks' predilection for the definite article in the names of rock bands. She was going out that night to see Gomez, and she allowed that this could only be a British group. "American bands are all the the the," she said. "The Replacements, the Beach Boys, the Dead. It's infuriating."

"Yes, of course," I replied, "and what about the Beatles, the Rolling Stones, the Who, the Animals, the Dave Clark Five, the Yardbirds, and the The (the amusing name under which Britisher Matt Johnson has chosen to release his musical efforts)? And what of Pearl Jam, Jefferson Airplane, Television, and Nine Inch Nails? They could all sing, in the words of (the article-less!) Grand Funk Railroad, 'We're an American band.' "

Needless to say, that wasn't me talking—that was *l'esprit d'escalier*. The trouble is, after I had formulated my perfectly worded rejoinder, I came to the conclusion that she had a point. Americans do have a thing for the word *the*. We say "in the hospital" and "in the spring"; the British sensibly omit the article. They favor collective or purely regional sports team names, such as Manchester United or Arsenal, while we have the New York Yankees, the Los Angeles Angels (which when you translate the Spanish becomes "the the Angels Angels"), and such syntactical curiosities as the Utah Jazz and the Orlando Magic. On the other hand, on the rare occasion when a British team is known by a plural, the article is omitted even though it appears to be necessary. To me, "Blackburn Rovers won the match," as you might read in (note absent *The*) *News of the World*, sounds like pidgin. Of course, this is coming from a person who, while working as a copyeditor, inserted a *the* in front of American Ballet Theatre. I was certain that the writer, who had covered dance for more than a decade, had made a thoughtless omission. My bad. American Ballet Theatre is indeed the name. Must have been founded by a Brit.

You could construct a whole course in American literature consisting of great novels whose titles start with the definite article: *The Deerslayer*, *The Scarlet Letter*, *The Red Badge of Courage*, *The Portrait of a Lady*, *The Great Gatsby*, *The Hamlet*, *The Old Man and the Sea*, *The Member of the Wedding*, *The Ghostwriter*, *The Color Purple*, *The Corrections*, and *The Da Vinci Code*. (Just kidding about that last one.) If British and Irish writers were as tied to this formula, they would have given us such works as *The Midsummer Night's Dream*, *The Christmas Carol*, *The Heart of Darkness*, *The Dubliners*, *The Vile Bodies*, *The Lord of the Flies*, *The Atonement*, and *The White Teeth*.

The creators of *Seinfeld* both mocked and participated in this convention. From the 5th episode to the 181st and last, every single episode of the series was dubbed *The* something, including such puzzling formulations as "The Serenity Now," "The Yada Yada," and "The Abstinence."

The British journalist Gilbert Adair has griped about American writers' and moviemakers' habit of *doubling* the definite article in titles like *The Bad and the Beautiful*, *The Pride and the Passion*, *The Naked and the Dead*, and *The Sound and the Fury*—which, if Faulkner had faithfully followed the Shakespearean quotation, would have been called *Sound and Fury*. (Graham Greene did title a novel *The Power and the Glory*, but he was faithfully quoting

The Book of Common Prayer, which is partial to the definite article.) If Jane Austen had used this construction, Adair pointed out, her most famous novel would be *The Pride and the Prejudice*—which "sounds like some best-selling bodice-ripper about the love of a cotton planter for a beautiful mulatress in the antebellum south." Ouch. But I'll point out that a recent trend in American movies is to drop the expected definite article, even if the source material has one. Maybe the Hollywood types think this will save money on ink, but whatever the reason, *Flight of the Phoenix*, *War of the Worlds*, *Bad News Bears*, *Wedding Crashers*, and *Fantastic Four* all recently played at my local multiplex. Also, the greatest American novel has no article, though it's often given one by misguided folks who, like me in my American Ballet Theatre blunder, think they're fixing a mistake. Mark Twain's title was, simply, *Adventures of Huckleberry Finn*.

Getting back to the definite article in names of musical groups, I hypothesize that the custom originated, quite logically, in the nomenclature of collective ensembles: the London Symphony, the Berlin Philharmonic, the Paul Whiteman Orchestra, the Quintet of the Hot Club of France (Django Reinhardt's outfit, and my nominee for the best group name of all time). *The + plural noun* names (along the lines of the Beatles, in which each member is referred to as *singular noun*, as in "Paul is the cute Beatle") require a bit more of an imaginative leap—and an American one, as my friend somehow sensed. In 1869, the first professional baseball team began play in Cincinnati. They wore red stockings, and through a process of synecdoche (the figure of speech where the part stands for the whole) they were called the Red Stockings. Fast-forward thirty-eight years, to 1907, when an a cappella singing group called the Growlers is formed at Yale; two years later it evolves into the Whiffenpoofs. The naming formula was well established by 1919, when an African-American group, the Four Harmony Kings, was recording. In 1924, jazz cornettist Bix Beiderbecke started the Wolverines. Round about 1930, Bob Wills played with the Light Crust Doughboys and the Aladdin Laddies, and then put together the Texas Playboys. The Inkspots began harmonizing shortly thereafter, siring the myriad doo-wop, rhythm and blues, and rock and roll combos of the fifties, which almost all had *the + plural noun* names and which collectively formed the Beatles' musical landscape.

In the first flush of Beatlemania, calling your band the Somethings seemed obligatory. But not long afterward, musicians started broadening their appellational horizons. The Who, followed by the Grateful Dead, the Velvet Underground, and the Band, reverted to collective nouns, and nearly all the "rock" (as opposed to rock and roll) bands of the late sixties and the seventies dispensed with the article altogether: Pink Floyd, Led Zeppelin, Traffic, Procol Harum, Cream, Deep Purple, Boston, Genesis, Aerosmith, etc., etc. The punk and new wave movements starting in the late seventies, as part of an effort to overthrow pretension and get back to rock's roots, brought back the article with a vengeance: the Clash, the Jam, the Sex Pistols, the Ramones, the New York Dolls, the B-52s. The batch after that tended to go without: Simply Red, Culture Club, Duran Duran, Spandau Ballet, Nirvana, U2, Gomez, and so on. Now it seems that one can go either way, with *the* names providing a slightly ironic nod to garage-band simplicity, article-less names going more in the direction of "art," and a few toying with expectations, such as Talking Heads, Eels, Doves, and Eurythmics (no *the* in any of them—the last is named after a theory of music education), the National (which makes us wonder, "The National *what*?"), and the The, which its founder, Matt Johnson, has described as "an antiname. You've got THE Damned, THE Clash, THE this, THE that and it's all the. There's so many ways it can be taken but it isn't a joke name, it's not self-mocking, it's sarcastic!"

I know of only two bands that start their name with an A, the eighties group A Flock of Seagulls and the hip-hop collective A Tribe Called Quest. That's no surprise. In almost every context, *a* has a dramatically lower profile than *the*. A (deriving from the Old English *an*, meaning the number one) implies the generic, which we shun; *the* implies the unique, which we crave. But the generic has its value and its charms. William Carlos Williams knew exactly what he was doing when he began his most famous poem: "so much depends/upon/a red wheel/barrow." Louis Zukofsky spent much of his life putting additions on a sprawling poem called, simply, A. Critic Hugh Kenner described this work as "an exegesis of the indefinite article, and so of cases standing for kinds, and so of a tension between the kind of reality kinds have and the stubborn intuition that your need for a filing system has merely devised them." The thousands and thousands of films, plays, and novels whose titles begin with *The* blare their own specialness; the handful of A titles (rare even in Britain) express an appealing and intriguing indefiniteness: consider Robert Altman's *A Wedding* and Paul Mazursky's *An Unmarried Woman*, Stephen Sondheim's *A Little Night Music* and Eugene O'Neill's *A Moon for the Misbegotten*, John Knowles's *A*

Separate Peace, Anthony Burgess's *A Clockwork Orange*, V. S. Naipaul's *A Bend in the River*, and William Dean Howells's *A Modern Instance* and *A Hazard of New Fortunes*.

A's rightful literary place is in narrative. In the opening line of a novel, a story, or a fairy tale, as we begin to be told what happened once upon *a* time, the natural progression is to be introduced to *a* person and situation, and then gradually be filled in on their particularity. And so Hardy commences *Tess of the D'Urbervilles*: "On an evening in the latter part of May a middle-aged man was walking homeward." A common device, however, is to catch the reader's attention with an artificial familiarity, achieved by using either the definite article ("The boy with fair hair lowered himself down the last few feet of rock and began to pick his way towards the lagoon"—*Lord of the Flies*) or the characters' names ("Ursula and Gudrun Brangwen sat one morning in the window-bay of their father's house in Beldover, working and talking"—*Women in Love*).

A joke is an elemental narrative, and the definite article has not invaded its domain: it's always *a* guy, never *the* guy, who walks into a bar, and it's certainly never anybody with a name, except people called Seamus or Abe in horrible ethnic jokes. (Jokes, like the stage directions in play and movie scripts, also are always rendered in the present tense.)* The only acceptable variant in joke and anecdote telling is the determiner *this*—as in "I met this girl, and she . . ." And here's a tip for all you aspiring Shecky Greenes out there: a study funded by the National Science Foundation has found that listeners actually retain the content of a story better when the storyteller introduces important nouns with *this* instead of *a*.†

One nice thing about *a* is that it hardly ever falls victim to the sin of pretentiousness. This is not the case with its definite buddy. My wife had a friend who, when he got accepted into law school, took to announcing, "I am studying the law." We have all read too many interviews where actors call a schlocky movie "the piece" and say that the most important thing in their lives is "the work." Defying the risk of appearing ridiculous, certain institutions insist on the definite article, including *The* Championships (a.k.a. the Wimbledon tennis tour-

---

* An exception to both the indefinite article and present tense conventions is found in certain riddles (it's why *did*, not *does*, *the* chicken cross the road) and one-liners ("Did you hear about the dyslexic, agnostic insomniac? He lay awake all night wondering if there really was a Dog").

† I am serious. The study is titled "The Cataphoric Use of the Indefinite *This* in Spoken Narrative," and it was published in *Memory & Cognition* 17 (1989), 536–540.

nament); *The* George Washington University; *The* Queen's College, Oxford; *The* Church of Jesus Christ of Latter-day Saints; and *The* Ohio State University. Bob Wolfley of the *Milwaukee Journal-Sentinel* wrote a column fantasizing that Monday Night Football banned players who had gone to OSU from including the *the* in the school name during those weird video clips where players give their name, rank, and alma mater. The show's producer explained (in Wolfley's imagination), "*The* introduction of a definite article before the name of a school which requires no further specification is superfluous and makes *the* speaker sound moronic or part of some creepy fraternity. *The* practice, this practice, must come to an end, *the* end." An expensive brand of hooch similarly makes a point that it must properly be referred to as *the* Glenlivet; in fact, on its Web site the *THE* is capitalized. A friend recalls having an *extremely* pretentious pal in college who would tilt his head toward the bottle when he popped the cork, then say, "Did you hear that? That's the sound of the *the*." And that's the sound of me losing my lunch.

On the other hand, sometimes people make their insider status known by pointedly *dropping* the definite article. My teenaged daughters and their friends ask each other, "What are you doing for [not *the*] prom?" The uninitiated refer to *the* CIA, but true operatives do not.

Interviewed by Michael Moore for the film *Fahrenheit 9/11*, since-departed then–CIA director Porter Goss said, "It is true I was in CIA from approximately the late '50's to approximately the early '70's. And it's true I was a case officer, clandestine services office and yes I do understand the core mission of the business. I couldn't get a job with CIA today. I am not qualified."

When a name or nickname is prefixed with *the*, the result, theoretically, is gravitas and distinction: George Herman Ruth was the Babe, John Wayne the Duke, and Elvis Presley the King; Bruce Springsteen is the Boss, Randy Johnson is the Big Unit, and the Pope is, well, the Pope. But if the planets aren't aligned, the effect turns ironic and diminishing, as in *The Great Santini*, the Fonz, the Donald [Trump], and the fellow the *Seinfeld* characters are talking about when they say, "Gotta love the Drake" or "I hate the Drake." The character played by Jeff Bridges in the 1998 film *The Big Lebowski* seems to be displaying some level of irony about himself when he says: "I'm the Dude. So that's what you call me. You know, that, or, uh, His Dudeness, or, uh, Duder, or El Duderino if you're not into the whole brevity thing." (For more on *dude*, see the chapter on interjections.) I remember once speaking to an associate of Mickey Rooney's, trying to set up an interview; the man's constant reference to his boss as "the

Mick" was disconcerting. (The interview never panned out, so I don't know if the Mick would have referred to *Sugar Babies* as "the piece.") The apotheosis of this is the Richmeister, the *Saturday Night Live* character played by Rob Schneider who managed the copy room and obsessively showered his coworkers with nicknames, most of which started with *the*. Thus a guy named Randy became "the Randman," "the Rand-ster," "the Great Randino," "the Randipulator," and "the *Rand* Old Opry."

The is normally used, even by the Richmeister, to raise the stature of the noun it precedes, but it can also be meant or perceived as demeaning. A common habit of low-lying racists is to make references to "the blacks," as if the members of this group were homogeneous and monolithic. I happened to be present at an editiorial meeting of the British newspaper the *Guardian* in which the readers' editor, Ian Mayes, attempted to make the case that phrases like "the disabled" and "the blind" were similarly dehumanizing; instead, he argued, the paper should refer to "disabled people." Political correctness is far less advanced in the UK than in the U.S., and his plea was met with not a few bewildered looks.

In geographical place-names, the definite article is usually neither degrading nor uplifting but simply a matter of ellipsis—that is, we refer to "the Caucasus" (implying "Mountains") and "the Yukon" (implying "Territory"). The number of articled countries is shrinking fast. Britons used to refer to the Argentine and the Lebanon, and I remember when Congo, Ivory Coast, Sudan, and Ukraine all had *the*'s. Thankfully, the Netherlands and the Philippines are still with us, and the Gambia—the name of the country's major river— actually calls itself the Republic of the Gambia, as if sticking two *the*'s in there were a way not to lose one of them. The financial district of London has long been called the City, and that is also the way residents of New York and San Francisco (famous urban chauvinists) refer to their hometowns.* San Franciscans also have the odd habit of calling their neighborhoods things like the Haight and the Richmond. *Southern* Californians have their own distinctive geographical use of the definite article: they refer to numbered highways as "the 101" or "the 5." This formulation may have led to the naming of the most popular television program in my household, *The* O.C. O.C., of course,

---

* New York's case is complicated. A resident of the borough of Brooklyn says, "Let's go into the city" in reference to a trip to Manhattan. But if she is upstate (i.e., anywhere north of Yonkers) for the weekend, "Let's go back to the city" means a return home to Brooklyn.

stands for Orange County, California, but judging by the sometimes heated comments of Internet bloggers, no one who lives there actually uses a *the*. The show's creator, Josh Schwartz, does seem to have a special appreciation for the ironic effects of the definite article. Characters on the program call their grandmother the Nana and debate the relative merits of the Nevada cities the Vegas and the Reno.

Probably the single most ironic rendition of *the* is the word *teh*, which so offends Microsoft Word and other word-processing programs that they instantly transpose the second and third letters of it. (I managed to retain the word by typing *tehe*, then, when the sentence was over, deleting the second *e*. This allows the word to remain but doesn't do anything about the annoying squiggly red line under it.) In the in-group Internet slang known as Leet, *teh* is used as an intensifier, as in "He is teh lame" and "This is teh suck."

But I won't end on an ironic note. Indeed, I want to maintain the dignity of *the* because I have it on good authority that I may soon become one.

I'll explain. It all started when I read two separate articles in the *New York Times* not long ago. The first was about celebrities and Hollywood types involved in

George W. Bush's 2005 inauguration. The *Times* reported that these included

> Gloria Estefan, the Cuban-born singer; Hilary Duff, the singer; Gary Sinise, the actor; Don King, the boxing promoter; Darryl Worley, the singer; Jason Sehorn, the former football player; Ben Stein, the comedian; the Guy Lombardo Orchestra; and the Radio City Rockettes.

The other article was about notable alumni of Allardice High School in Pittsburgh, including:

> Tom Reich, a prominent baseball and hockey player agent; James Langer, a vice president of the National Academy of Sciences; Tom Roberts, the music director for the film "The Aviator"; Rob Marshall, a director; Marty Allen, a comedian . . .

It should be immediately clear that the main difference between the two lists of names is their use of the definite and indefinite article: the first one favors *the*, the second *a*. And the way the *Times* has listed the Allardice High School graduates makes sense. "The Aviator" had only one music director, so Tom Roberts properly gets a *the*, but there are presumably multiple vice presidents of the National Academy of Sciences, and there are definitely lots of directors, so James Langer and Rob Marshall each gets an *a*. But take a look at the Bush-liking celebrities. Singers (Cuban-born and otherwise), actors, boxing promoters, former football players, and comedians are all legion—so why do these folks qualify for a *the*?

I've always been impressed by the scene in *Annie Hall* in which the character played by Woody Allen, in the middle of an argument concerning Marshall McLuhan, produces the real McLuhan to settle the issue. In that spirit, I posed my question about *the* to the person best qualified to answer it: Allan M. Siegal, then the standards editor of the *Times* and the keeper of its style book. (He has since retired.) He e-mailed me back a detailed reply that began by quoting the style manual, which is available to the public under the title *The New York Times Manual of Style and Usage*: "In a reference to someone well known, a descriptive phrase preceded by *the* is acceptable: *the sociologist Merrill H. Cordero*." Then he amplified:

We have these options in referring to someone whose name is not quite a household word that stands alone:

1. Yo-Yo Ma, the cellist (which will irritate some readers who didn't think they needed to be told who Ma is).

2. Mark Smith, a cellist (making it absolutely clear that we think he's an unknown).

3. the cellist Yo-Yo Ma (which, interestingly, does not offend readers because by the time they read the name, they don't remember that we felt it necessary to supply a further identification).

4. Yo-Yo Ma, cellist (a form that used to appear in The Times for borderline cases, but now strikes us as too telegraphic).

5. cellist Yo-Yo Ma, which is favored by most newspapers (and Bill Safire) because it raises none of the foregoing objections. Legal papers almost invariably use "defendant Al Siegal." We still think that's unpolished usage.

I happen to agree that Number 5 is "unpolished usage"; I was troubled when a reference I made in my last book to "the English author Zadie Smith" was changed to "English author Zadie Smith." But it is extremely common and is sanctioned by the *Associated Press Style Guide*, among other authorities. In fact, the first sentence of a novel whose success is matched only by its wooden writing, *The Da Vinci Code*, reads: "Renowned curator Jacques Saunière staggered through the vaulted archway of the museum's Grand Gallery." An academic study—this one *not* funded by the National Academy of Sciences—investigated the prevalence of "determiner deletion," as the author called it, in major British newspapers: that is, whether the paper would write "the Australian entrepreneur Alan Bond" or merely "Australian entrepreneur Alan Bond." He found that the most upscale paper, the *Times*, deleted the article just 5 percent of the time, compared to 89 percent for the most downscale tabloid, the *Sun*. The construction was popularized and probably invented by *Time* magazine, whose founder, Henry Luce, promulgated a telegraphic style, subsequently known as *Time*-ese, that turned descriptions and job titles into capitalized and article-less Homeric epithets, including (I found all of these in a single issue from 1935): "Negro Pugilist Joe Louis," "slick-haired Researcher W. E. Ruder," "Cinemactress Katharine Hepburn," "long-faced Funnyman Joseph Francis ('Buster') Keaton," "baseball's Tsar Kenesaw Mountain Landis," and "cheerful psychotic Will Stevens."*

---

* Wolcott Gibbs's satiric 1936 *New Yorker* profile of "ambitious, gimlet-eyed, Baby Tycoon Henry Robinson Luce" pilloried this and other elements of *Time*-ese, including inverted construction and breathless punctuation. (The piece famously concluded, "Where it will end, knows God!") In the late 1980s, *Spy* magazine ironically nodded to the custom, using such epithets as "short-fingered vulgarian Donald Trump." Yet another ironic variation is what might be called the Letterman Possessive: the talk-show host will introduce guests as "television's Regis Philbin," "baseball's Alex Rodriguez," etc.

But I digress. The point is that the *Times* observes an *a/the* divide, crossed when a person becomes "well known." The system has a couple of problems. The first concerns the logic of Siegal's Number 1, "Yo-Yo Ma, the cellist," which you find a lot in the *Times*, but not, thankfully, many other places. I believe it stems from a legitimate comma-less formulation meant to differentiate two people with the same name. Thus, you might say, "Bill Bradley the former senator" to make it clear you're not speaking of Bill Bradley the ex–football player. Henry the Eighth isn't Henry the Seventh or Henry the Ninth, and none of them takes a comma. However, it is not really accurate to say, "Yo-Yo Ma, the cellist," as the *Times* habitually does, because he is not *the* cellist; there are other people who play the instrument.

I didn't want to come off as even more pedantic than I already appeared to be, so I resisted taking that up with Siegal. I asked him instead if the newspaper maintained a list of "well-known" people, and, in any event, how the decision is made whether an individual qualifies. I imagined a council of editors who met the first Monday of every month and weighed in: "Tom Reich: *a.* Don King: *the* . . ." No such animal, Siegal assured me. Copyeditors made the decisions "case by case, subject to sharpshooting after the fact."

Well, here's some sharpshooting. Marty "Hello Dere" Allen, the wacky, frizzy-haired half of the classic sixties comedy duo Allen and Rossi, is not *a* comedian. He is *the* comedian—at least as much as Ben Stein is, and as much as Jason Sehorn is *the* former football player or Darryl Worley (who may be well known but not to me) is *the* singer.

But I put this with all due respect, because I need to stay on the *Times'* good side. In the course of my e-mail correspondence with Siegal, I happened to mention that I was sure that if the *Times* ever had cause to refer to me, it would be as "Ben Yagoda, *a* writer." He replied, on the contrary, that he was already starting to think of me as a *the*, and added:

"I trust your next book will place you in that category."

Memo to the comedian Marty Allen: once I'm on the inside, I'll make things right.

CHAPTER IV

Conj. Int. N.
Prep. Pron. V.
Adj. Adv. Art.

Must it all be either less or more,
Either plain or grand?
Is it always "or"?
Is it never "and"?
That's what woods are for:
For those moments in the woods . . .

Let the moment go.
Don't forget it for a moment, though.
Just remembering you've had an "and," when you're
    back to "or,"
Makes the "or" mean more than it did before.

—*Stephen Sondheim, "Moments in the Woods"*

Conjunctions, at least as they've been traditionally defined, are almost as murky a speech part as adverbs.
There are two main categories. The coordinating conjunctions are the well-known workhorses *and*, *or*, and
but (with *nor*, *for*, *so*, and *yet* playing cameo roles); they

connect sentence elements—nouns, adjectives, verbs, clauses, whatever—to each other. *Because, although, until, after, as, before, like, since, that, than, while, since, if, for, that,* and a bunch of others are known as subordinating conjunctions. They link only clauses, and the clause following the conjunction in some way depends on, or is subordinate to, the other clause in the sentence. "People eat *because* they're hungry." "I'll go *if* you go." "My guests arrived *before* I did."

The subordinating conjunctions are definitely important. As Daniel Duncan wrote in *A New English Grammar* in 1731, "It is the good or bad Use of Conjunction, that constitutes the Essence of a good or bad Stile. They render the Discourse more smooth and fluent. They are the Helpmates of Reason in arguing, relating and putting the other Parts of Speech in due order." But as a category, they have always been pretty funky, in part because so many of them are used in other contexts as other parts of speech. The muddle led even the reliably lucid H. W. Fowler to commit such murky sentences as "Many words are sometimes conjunctions and sometimes adverbs—*therefore, so, however, since,* etc.—and such words as *when* and *where,* though often in effect conjunctions, are more strictly described as relative adverbs with expressed or implied antecedent." In 2002, Huddleston and Pullum's *Cambridge Grammar* pretty much blew the subordinating conjunctions out of the water. The book's lineup of "lexical categories" (for H and P, "parts of speech" and "word classes" were both passé terms) includes the "coordinator," which was just another name for the coordinating conjunctions. However, their "subordinator" class consists of just five words: *that* ("I hope that you're coming"), *for* ("that's the best course for you to take), *to* ("I want you to come"), *whether*, and *if* (in the sense of *whether*). *Because*, *until*, and all the rest? They were reclassified as prepositions.

If you want to read their explanation, it's on pages 1011 through 1014. Suffice it to say that it works for me. Like the articles *a* and *the*, the classic conjunctions (or coordinators) *and*, *but*, and *or* provide plenty of meat to chew on. But let me, before moving on to them, spend a moment on the part of speech formerly known as subordinating conjunctions. They're a bit like an exclusive country club: a lot of other words really want to get in. The classic example is *like*. It could be argued that what started modern American grammatical prescriptivism, which flowered in the seventies and eighties in the persons of Wilson Follett, John Simon, Edwin Newman, and Jacques Barzun, was the mid-1950s cigarette ad campaign that featured the slogan "Winston tastes good—like a cigarette should."

The use of the preposition *like* instead of the subordinating conjunction *as* outraged grammar mavens; legions of baby boomers remember this mistake being used as an object lesson in their junior high school English classes and dinner table conversations. Winston, far from being ashamed of the error, reveled in it, following up with another commercial in which a woman with her gray hair in a bun objects to the wording. A mob of smokers responds, "What do you want, good grammar or good taste?" (The brand happily continued with the anti-elitist tack, eventually adopting the slogan "Me and my Winstons . . . we got a real good thing," which commits an impressive four crimes against standard usage in just ten words. Another brand jumped on the bandwagon as well, with the slogan "Us Tareyton smokers would rather fight than switch.")

At this point, assuming you believe subordinating conjunctions exist, *like* has made it into the club. Robert Burchfield's recent edition of *Fowler's Modern English Usage*, which gamely navigates the waters between prescriptivism and descriptivism, okays four separate conjunctive uses of the word. In my view, the first three are fine in conversation. In fact, they're better than fine, as you can see by their sterling use in song lyrics: 1) *like* meaning "in the way that" ("If you knew Susie like I know Susie"—Eddie Cantor, and "Why don't you love me like you used to do?"—Hank Williams); 2) *like* meaning "as if" or "as though" ("She acts like we never have met"—Bob Dylan); and 3) *like* meaning "just as" ("Tell it like it is"—Otis Redding). But I have a problem with the fourth, *like* meaning simply *as*, as in "Like I said, I want to go home." My problem is less grammatical than behavioral. This tends to be a favorite locution of bores and boors and it always makes me want to ask, "If you already said it, why are you saying it again?"

Another group of wannabe conjunctions consists of such sentence adverbs as *however*, *therefore*, and *unfortunately*. I know this because I correct hundreds of student written assignments a year, and roughly half contain a sentence along the lines of "I enjoy going to school, however, some days I just want to sleep in." *However*, in other words, is being used as an equivalent of *but*, with which it can easily be replaced (the comma after the word being removed in the process). If the student really wants to keep *however*, the comma after "school" has to be changed to a period or semicolon. I dutifully make these marks on the papers, with the sense that I am pursuing a lost cause. *However* and its brethren are chugging toward the conjunction junction and will arrive any day now.

In books on usage and style, the most frequent comment you find about conjunctions is something to the effect that despite what other books on usage and style say, it's acceptable to start sentences with the words *and* and *but*. But this is a classic straw man: there *is* no book containing such a prohibition. The closest thing I've seen is a quotation from a nineteenth-century grammarian named George Washington Moon, dug up by scholar Dennis Baron. Moon wrote: "It is not scholarly to begin a sentence with the conjunction *and*." And it probably *isn't* scholarly, but in most other kinds of writing it's perfectly fine, as is kicking off with the conjunctions *but, yet, nor, for* ("For in that sleep of death what dreams may come . . . must give us pause"—*Hamlet*), and *so.* That word brings to mind one of the things I was taught in junior high school that really stuck—Mrs. Reddington's remark that in Shakespeare's day, there were no fancy props, so the text had to do the work of stage settings. And that's why, in *As You Like It*, Rosalind opens a scene by saying: "So this is the Forest of Arden."* In 1963, re-

---

* *Or* is a bit trickier. It can start off an interrogative sentence, as in the lyricist Jimmy Van Heusen's "Or would you like to swing on a star?" but in nonfragmentary declarative sentences, it seems to really want to be followed by some kind of modifier. "Or, on the other hand, he might be a man heretofore doomed to peace and obscurity, but, in reality, made to shine in war."—Crane, *The Red Badge of Courage.*

searcher Francis Christensen analyzed the work of a group of unassailable writers including H. L. Mencken, Lionel Trilling, and Edmund Wilson and found they began 8.75 percent of their sentences with *and* or *but*. *And* also seems to be a good way to commence catchphrases and slogans, including "And away we go" (Jackie Gleason), "And that's the way it is" (Walter Cronkite), "And now for something completely different" (Monty Python), "And that's the truth" (Lily Tomlin's character Edith Anne), "And so it goes" (Kurt Vonnegut's *Slaughterhouse Five*), and "And one!" (basketball announcers' shorthand for when a player is fouled in the process of making a shot, now the name for a giant sports apparel company).

Many, many sentences in the King James Bible start with *and*—so many that such sentence constructions now have a strong biblical feel. That is one reason why William Blake's untitled lines from the preface to his poem "Milton" were later so successfully adapted as the hymn "Jerusalem." It begins:

> *And did those feet in ancient time*
> *Walk upon England's mountains green?*
> *And was the holy Lamb of God*
> *On England's pleasant pastures seen?*
> *And did the Countenance Divine*

> *Shine forth upon our clouded hills?*
> *And was Jerusalem builded here*
> *Among those dark Satanic mills?*

Still, you can go too far with this. Sixteen sentences in George H. W. Bush's 1989 inaugural address, for example, started with *and*, including these three in a row, about John Tower: "And he's a true expert on defense policy. And he understands the challenges ahead. And he's established great credibility." One suddenly understands that all those high school composition teachers probably meant that you shouldn't start *succeeding* sentences with *and*, lest you sound like a small child describing his day at the beach: "And we got ice cream. And Julie got sunburned. And a big wave came." Etc. (*Etc.*, by the way, is an abbreviation for the Latin *et cetera*, which means "and others of the same kind." Therefore, you should not put an *and* before it.)

Incidentally, I know of one way to *end* a sentence with this word. It's an expression I associate with a certain long-gone period in the life of New York when there was Chock Full o' Nuts instead of Starbucks, and it usually came in the form of a question or a suggestion: "Let's go out for coffee and." Could be a bagel, could be a Danish, could just be conversation, and it's an offer I still find very hard to refuse. People also end sentences with *but*, followed by an unspoken ellipsis to indicate an unspoken qualification: "He's good looking, but . . ." In Australian and New Zealand slang, a final *but* means "though" or "however," as in "Yes, I told 'im. Not the whole of it, but."

Something about *and*—probably its utter indispensability—has made it prone to being represented by other means than just the standard three letters. The plus sign is a favorite of instant messagers, note takers, hip-hop songwriters, conglomerates (Gulf + Western), and people demonstrating eternal love by carving their initials into trees. A little more elegant is the ampersand (&), which dates from the first century and is a ligature, or combination, of the letters *e* and *t* (*and* in Latin) into a single symbol. It was included in systems of typography starting in the fifteenth century, and ever since has been the character into which a type designer can inject the most artistic flair. The *word* "ampersand" didn't come into being until the nineteenth century. At that time *&* was customarily taught as the twenty-seventh letter of the alphabet and pronounced "and." When schoolchildren recited their ABCs, they concluded with the words "and, per se [i.e., by itself], 'and.'" This eventually became corrupted to "ampersand." The symbol is a favorite of law and architecture firms, and is invaluable in parsing screenplay credits. For example, the script for

the 1989 ampersand-titled film *Turner & Hooch* is credited to "Dennis Shyrack & Michael Blodgett and Daniel
Petrie Jr. and Jim Cash & Jack Epps Jr." This is not
the result of haphazard typography. Rather, following
Writers Guild of America guidelines, it indicates that
Messrs. Shyrack and Blodgett and Messrs. Cash and
Epps worked as teams, and that they and Mr. Petrie each
contributed separate drafts of the screenplay. A good
rule of thumb is that the more ampersands in the credits, the crummier the movie.

Presumably in an attempt to mimic speech, where
the word is frequently swallowed, people writing *and*
sometimes leave out the first and third letters. This creates problems, specifically in the matter of apostrophes.
If you want to replace the *and* in "rock and roll" with
the letter *n*, by all rights you should put apostrophes before and after it, to stand in for the missing letters, the
way we use the apostrophe in *isn't* to indicate the absent
o. This is far—very far—from the only way it is done,
however. A brief survey of the Internet finds the following variations: Rock 'n' roll. Rock'n'roll (no spaces).
Rock n roll. Rock-n-roll. Rock 'n roll. Rock n' roll.
Such appellational cacophony can be expected, possibly even embraced, because the term is in the public
domain. The surprising thing is that even when multi-
national corporations register trade names of this sort,

apostrophe placement appears whimsical. Thus in a tour of the supermarket one encounters Shake 'n Bake, Sweet'N Low, Wash'n Dri, and Light n' Lively. I don't know of any company that uses both apostrophes. Maybe they're trying to save on ink, too.*

As far as meaning is concerned, *and* would seem to be pretty simple: an agent for combining words, phrases, and clauses. That it is, but it is not simply the verbal equivalent of a plus sign. It can bring additional meaning to the party, at times implying causation ("Jones had the best presentation and got the account") or sequence ("He got in the car and drove to work"). *And* serves as an intensifier in expressions like "nice and easy" and "when I'm good and ready." When it doubles certain words, it sug-

---

*Another vexing issue has to do with the orientation of the apostrophe. Most typography systems use the closed single quotation mark (') to represent an apostrophe. On typewriter keyboards, there are no closed and open single quotation marks, merely a single vertical mark used for both of them and for apostrophes. There is likewise only one key for these three symbols on computer keyboards, but word processing programs *display* open and closed quotation marks and believe that they can divine which one the user wants. They believe wrong. For example, Microsoft Word forces me to write "Rock 'n' Roll" (with the first apostrophe not an apostrophe at all) unless I do some fancy rejiggering. This error is widely seen in print advertising, most commonly in ads for '98 Plymouths and the like.

gests different kinds of intensification: "he got bigger and bigger"; "the car went faster and faster"; "we walked and walked"; "the meeting lasted hours and hours." In Robert Browning's "Alack, there be roses and roses," *and* is used to imply the existence of two or more very different categories of the flower. The expressions *try and*, *come and*, and *go and* are sometimes vilified (the *and*s should supposedly be replaced by *to*s) but are perfectly acceptable in conversation and all but the most elevated prose, and have been for some time: "her constant hypocrisy is to try and make her girls believe that her father is a respectable man"— William Thackeray, *The Book of Snobs*, 1846. (Not to mention the question Mae West asked Cary Grant in the 1933 film *She Done Him Wrong*: "Why don't you come up some time and see me?"*) The word is also used in the idiomatic exclamations "And how!" and "and then some," as well as the peculiarly American "and all," seen in William Carlos Williams's wonderful title "Spring and All," and invoked by J. D. Salinger's Holden Caulfield at least once a page, including in the image that inspires the novel's title: "Anyway, I keep picturing all these little kids playing some game in this big field of rye and all."

---

* This is almost universally misquoted as "Why don't you come up and see me some time," which is what W. C. Fields said to West in the 1939 *My Little Chickadee*.

The classical rhetorical figure polysyndeton is the stringing together of *and*s in a sentence. It is used most famously in Macbeth's "Tomorrow, and tomorrow, and tomorrow/Creeps in this petty pace from day to day," but most frequently in the King James Bible—for example, in the Lord's Prayer: "For thine is the kingdom, and the power, and the glory, for ever and ever." The modern master, of course, is Hemingway; entrants in Bad Hemingway contests would be lost without it. But they rarely if ever attain the mood of the original, seen, for example, in the short story "After the Storm": "It wasn't about anything, something about making punch, and then we started fighting and I slipped and he had me down kneeling on my chest and choking me with both hands like he was trying to kill me and all the time I was trying to get the knife out of my pocket to cut him loose."

The complexity of *and* multiplies when you think of it alongside its cousin *or*. *Or* is technically disjunctive, rather than conjunctive, meaning that usually, of the two or more possibilities it separates, only one is accurate, operative, necessary, or possible. In other words, when *or* is used, the word *either* is understood to precede it: "Ninth-grade students may take [either] cooking or art." But confusion is possible. *Or* sometimes is not disjunctive but explanatory, meaning something like *that is*: "He is the provost, or the chief academic officer, of the university." And in certain constructions, *or* means exactly the same thing as *and*: Sentence one: "The dessert choices are ice cream or cake." Sentence two: "The dessert choices are ice cream and cake." Some wise guys, when asked, "Would you like ice cream or cake?" answer, "Yes." They do this because a) they're hungry and b) *or* has yet another wrinkle. Sometimes when it's used, the significant idea is merely that *one* (doesn't matter which) of the items separated by it is operative. Travel agent to customer: "I know you requested an oceanside room, but would poolside or mountainside be acceptable?"

Rules, guidelines, and requirements are the places where confusion with *and* and *or* is most likely to come up, especially when negatives are involved. A set of logical principles known as DeMorgan's Rules holds:

Not (a and b) = not a or not b
Not (a or b) = not a and not b

A recent article in the *New York Times* got messed up by DeMorgan's Rules, as a subsequent correction acknowledged:

[The original piece] misstated the third rule for robots from "I, Robot," by the science-fiction author

Isaac Asimov, a guideline for their coexistence with humans. (Asimov's first two rules were "Do not hurt humans" and "Obey humans unless that violates Rule 1.") His third rule was, "Defend yourself unless that violates Rule 1 OR Rule 2"—not "Rule 1 AND Rule 2."

It's a big difference. As the *Times* originally had it, a robot could defend itself in a case where an alien was attacking it and a human had forbidden it to move; but in Asimov's conception, it could not. A further wrinkle occurs when *and* implies, as it often does, simultaneity. Saying that people shouldn't drink and drive is sensible; saying that they shouldn't drink or drive would change life as we know it.

Not surprisingly, the inherent complexities posed by the two short words have caused problems in the law— so much so that New York State has a statute, known as the and/or rule, stating: "Generally, the words 'or' and 'and' in a statute may be construed as interchangeable when necessary to effectuate legislative intent." (Many other states have similar measures.) In other words, when convenient, *or* can mean *and* and *and* can mean *or*! It's a pity that neither George Orwell nor Lewis Carroll lived to see the and/or rule. In his book *The Language of Judges*, Lawrence Solon describes a case where it was applied. Here are the facts of the case, as described by the court:

> On February 20, 1972 the complaining police officer stopped the defendant for a traffic infraction and while writing the tickets the defendant approached and argued with the officer. He was advised by the officer to go back to his car but returned again. At this time the defendant stated that the officer could shove the summons up his f—— a——. In response to the officer's questioning "What did you say?" the invective was repeated. At this time the officer alighted from his car and again directed the defendant to return to his vehicle. Again the defendant is alleged to have stated, "Go f—— yourself" and in response to the officer's inquiry repeated the words.

The defendant was arrested on charges of harassment. New York law holds that a person is guilty of harassing another person when "he engages in a course of conduct *or* repeatedly commits acts which alarm or seriously annoy such other person and which serve no legitimate purpose" (emphasis added). The defendant was acquitted because the court, using the and/or rule, interpreted *or* to mean *and*, meaning that the defendant would have had to *repeatedly* commit annoying acts, which he did not.

The and/or rule should not be confused with the term *and/or*, which originated in mercantile and shipping law in the nineteenth century, when it was rendered like a numerical fraction, with the *and* on top of a horizontal line and the *or* beneath it. The first use in normal typography cited by the *OED* dates from 1916. *And/or* neutralizes the disjunctiveness of *or* and means, or should mean, "option A, option B, or both." (There is no term that conveys the idea of "option A, option B, or neither." It's something flight attendants could use when they wheel around the beverage cart and ask, "Coffee or tea?" Instead, they communicate the no-beverage option with a slight rising of the voice on the word *tea*. Their voice would descend on the word if passengers were required to drink.) But in other than the simplest contexts *and/or* is prone to ambiguity and/or abuse that has roused many legal commentators to states of vigorous condemnation. In his authoritative *The Language of the Law*, David Melinkoff calls *and/or* "an unfortunate expression" guilty of "clouding the law." He cites a will that left a gift to "A and/or B" and a contract containing the following language: "and shall not in manner or form be construed to be a partnership and/or limited partnership relationship"; in both cases, *and/or* is, as Melinkoff says, meaningless.

Outside the law, *and/or*, admittedly, is not the most

graceful term—Fowler says it "should not be allowed." But if you're pressed for time, it's useful shorthand for giving the idea of *a or b or both*. Its air of official precision also lends it comic potential. Chuck Klosterman writes of being asked to write an article for *Spin* magazine visiting the places where famous rock-related deaths occurred, and to give it an "epic" quality. He later wrote, "This, obviously, is a strange request. The word 'epic' is not often used in the offices of *Spin*, except in the context of measuring co-workers' public meltdowns and/or describing people's drinking problems."

In the language of logic, as opposed to the language of English, *and/or* is unnecessary because *or* in itself denotes *a or b or both*. Non-logicians have become acquainted with this idea in recent years, with the advent of computer database searches, especially of the World Wide Web. Early on, it was decided that such searches would employ what is known as Boolean logic. That is, if you searched for *big OR juicy*, you would be presented with all documents that mentioned *big* or *juicy* or both, while *big AND juicy* would deliver only ones that mentioned both terms. Boolean logic employs additional conjunctions that would be quite useful in English. *New NOT York* will give you all mentions of *New*, minus the ones that also mention *York*, "New York" looks for the exact phrase, and *New w/10 York* finds instances where *New* and *York* are used within ten words of each other. *Or* obviously provides the most hits, and in the early days of the Internet it was the default connector; that is, if you typed *New York* into a search engine like Alta Vista, it would, on its own, insert an *or* between the two words and proceed accordingly. With the incredible expansion of the Web, narrow searches became more sought after than broad ones, and *and* has replaced *or* as the default conjunction.

As opposed to *and* and *or*, which link verbal elements, *but* distinguishes them—indicating that what follows is in opposition to ("I'd like to go to the fair, but I can't"), is a refinement of ("The statements was interesting, but tough"—Huck Finn, on his reading of *Pilgrim's Progress*), departs from ("But enough about me"), or flat out contradicts ("It was not black but white") what came before. It also can mean something like *except* or *other than*, for example in such sentences as "I could not but bow my head." This sounds old-fashioned because so many people now say, "I could not help but bow my head," which technically makes no sense but at least doesn't sound antiquated. *But* also shows up in peculiar idioms, including exclamations like "My, but you've grown" and the intensifying way Jimmy Van Heusen used it in the song "But Beautiful."

But is an extremely useful word. But it sometimes appears to be more useful than it actually is. Harold Ross (him again!) was religiously opposed to what he called the "meaningless but" in such phrases as "neat but gaudy" and "tall but sad": that is, *but*s implying a nonexistent opposition or contradiction. A Web writer with the piquant handle "Does This Blog Make My Butt Look Big?" recently posted this:

> A commentator on the news this morning . . . said that "a car bomb blew up in Iraq, killing five people, but none were Americans." Doesn't the wording of this sentence—namely the use of the *but* conjunction—imply that the murder of 5 people is somehow less terrible if no Americans are among the dead?

Indeed it does.

But is nearly irresistible to people who write legal briefs, campaign speeches, and op-ed pieces. I turn to the opinion page of this morning's *Philadelphia Inquirer* and find a column by Froma Harrop in which seven of the forty-nine sentences—more than 14 percent—begin with the word. She writes, for example, "We could crush oil's power to hurt us with a serious campaign to kick our fossil-fuel habit. But we don't, because we have an administration and Congress that care more about the oil industry than about us." This *but* is typical in adding nothing semantically; her meaning would be exactly the same without it. However, by emphasizing the contrast between what we could and what we actually do, it greases the wheels of the argument.

But sometimes there is no contrast and no opposition, and *but* merely provides the appearance of argumentation. That's true of at least three of the dozens of sentences John Kerry started with *but* in his foreign policy debate with George W. Bush in October 2004:

- What I think troubles a lot of people in our country is that the president has just sort of described one kind of mistake. But what he has said is that, even knowing there were no weapons of mass destruction, even knowing there was no imminent threat, even knowing there was no connection with Al Qaeda, he would still have done everything the same way.

- I'm going to get it right for those soldiers, because it's important to Israel, it's important to America, it's important to the world, it's important to the fight on terror. But I have a plan to do it.

- And our goal in my administration would be
  to get all of the troops out of there with a
  minimal amount you need for training and
  logistics as we do in some other countries in the
  world after a war to be able to sustain the peace.
  But that's how we're going to win the peace, by
  rapidly training the Iraqis themselves.

Politicians and other ideologues seem to feel the
word has magical powers, and maybe it does. I remember watching *Perry Mason* as a kid. Some suspicious
character would be on the stand testifying that he was
not at the Blue Bird Motel on the night of June 6. Then
Perry would say, "But is it not a fact that you *were* at the
Blue Bird Motel on the night of June 6?" The poor
schmo would immediately break down and confess that
he was there, and that he did a lot of other bad things
as well.

My first job was as an assistant editor of the *New
Leader*, a political biweekly whose contributors' articles
were studded with *but*s, like cloves in a ham. Most of
them did not survive, however. Myron "Mike" Kolatch,
the editor of the magazine, was religiously opposed to
word repetition, and especially vigilant about use of this
conjunction more than two or at the most three times in
an article. Consequently, *but* management was one of

the most important tasks of assistant editors. In short order I developed a list of substitutes that I could mentally summon in a flash. I can still run through them at a dinner party when the conversation lags: *yet*, *though*, *however*, *nevertheless* (or *nonetheless*—both couldn't be used in the same piece), *still*, and, getting more baroque, *albeit*, *at the same time*, *by the same token*, and *be that as it may*.

But word variation did not make for the best prose; how could it, when unfortunate concoctions like *by the same token* were part of the mix? When I was researching a book on *The New Yorker*, I found a 1940s memo that one of the magazine's writers, St. Clair McKelway, had written to William Shawn, then the editor for nonfiction (and eventually Ross's successor as editor in chief). In a profile of Walter Winchell, McKelway had opened a couple of sentences with *but* and Shawn, possibly for word-repetition reasons, had changed them; for example, "But love is tricky" was turned into "However, love is tricky." McKelway made an impassioned defense of *but*:

> If you are trying for an effect which comes from having built up a small pile of pleasant possibilities which you then want to push over as quickly as possible, dashing the reader's hopes that he is going to get out of a nasty situation as easily as you have in-

tentionally led him to believe, you have got to use the word "but" and it is usually more effective if you begin the sentence with it. "But love is tricky" means one thing, and "However, love is tricky" means another—or at least gives the reader a different sensation. However indicates a philosophical sigh; but presents an insuperable obstacle. . . . But, when used as I used it in these two places, is, as a matter of fact, a wonderful word. In three letters it says a little of however, and also be that as it may, and also here's something you weren't expecting and a number of other phrases along that line. There is no substitute for it. It is short and ugly and common. But I love it.

Four decades later, *The New Yorker* was still trying to cut down on *buts*, but for a different reason. When I interviewed the essayist Adam Gopnik for a different book, *The Sound on the Page*, he told me that when he started writing art criticism for the magazine in the 1980s, he had a difficult time making the transition from the academic papers he was used to. "The natural tone in graduate school is argumentative, and one result of that was my sentences tended to have a lot of *buts* in them," he said. "[*New Yorker* editor] Chip McGrath said to me, 'You have enough *buts* in here to form six human beings.' He taught me to write with *and* instead of *but*. Doing that leads to a somewhat disingenuous stance—you're still being argumentative, but it's disguised as a train of linked observations. I became more attractive to readers."

This kind of thinking could make you more attractive to human beings, too. Psychotherapist D. Wilson Johns imagines a mother saying to her daughter, "That is a nice picture, Jenny, but mommy doesn't have time right now to watch you draw." Too much of this, Johns advises, and Jenny will develop a complex. The reason, he writes, is that "the word 'but' negates or discounts what comes before it. If I say, 'I love you *but* I don't want to talk about it,' the listener tends to hear the last part of the conjunction and miss the first part." Like Gopnik, Johns favors substituting *and* whenever possible, and, to help readers remember, quotes a maxim devised by his father, H.D.: "Scratch your buts."

CHAPTER V

Int.

N. Prep. Pron. V. Adj. Adv. Art. Conj.

CLAUDIO: O, what men dare do! what men may do!
what men daily do, not knowing what they do!
BENEDICK: How now! interjections? Why, then,
some be of laughing, as, ah, ha, he!
—*Shakespeare*, Much Ado About Nothing, *Act IV, Scene 1*

Any unified theory of interjections—the words that, all by
themselves, express reactions or emotions or serve other
purposes in discourse—would have to start, like much else,
with *The Simpsons*. And any discussions of interjections in
The Simpsons would have to start with Homer's trademark
D'oh—the "annoyed grunt" (as it's designated in Simpsons
scripts and episode titles) that is his response to any big or
small adversity. One of the striking things about the word
is its speed of utterance, which is about the same as the
self-inflicted forehead smack that often accompanies it.
D'oh started out quite differently. Dan Castellaneta, the
voice of Homer, modeled his original rendition on James
Finlayson, the master of the "slow burn" in silent and early

sound comedies, many with Laurel and Hardy. Whenever angered or exasperated, Finlayson would let out a protracted "Dooooooh." However, Matt Groening, the creator of *The Simpsons*, felt this wasn't suited to the pace of animation. The rest is interjection history.

D'oh gets most of the attention, but *The Simpsons* features—you could almost say is defined by—many other interjections. Homer says "Ooooh" when an amorous thought occurs to him, and when he is about to eat something desirable, he makes an "Mmmmm" sound, usually followed by the name of the item: for example, "Mmmmm, crumpled-up cookie things," "Mmmmm, open-faced club sandwiches," and (after tasting some beef jerky) "Mmmmm, salty." Simpsons characters say "Yoinks" when they take or snatch something and "Woo-hoo" to express celebration or joy. The last, maybe even more than *D'oh*, is the Simpsons interjection most commonly uttered by real people. Like *whoopee*, *yippee*, *wow*, Archie Bunker's *whoop-de-doo*, and other such words, it's commonly said sarcastically, the attitude emphasized by an infixer: *Woo-freaking-hoo.**

---

* *The Simpsons* may have popularized this expression, but the show didn't originate it. The ever-reliable *OED* offers this line of dialogue from a 1915 novel by Gene Stratton-Porter: "Whoohoo it's so good, Mickey!"

The Archie Bunker example is a reminder that while *The Simpsons* may be the exemplar, television in general is a kind of interjection petri dish. Even the Capri-pants-wearing (Laura) Petrie dish, Mary Tyler Moore on *The Dick Van Dyke Show*, had a trademark one-word cry: "Rooooooobbb!" Consider, as well: "Aaaayh" and "Correctamundo" (the Fonz); "Awww" (the studio audience of any show at a touching or romantic moment); "Bam" (Chef Emeril Lagasse); "Cowabunga" (in three separate incarnations—Chief Thunderthud on *The Howdy-Doody Show*, the Teenage Mutant Ninja Turtles, and Bart Simpson); "Dy-no-mite" (Jimmy "J.J." Walker); "Gollee" and "Shazam" (Gomer Pyle—the latter borrowed from Captain Marvel); "Heh-heh-heh-heh" (Beavis and Butthead); "Hey, hey, hey" (Fat Albert); "Hey now" (Hank on *The Larry Sanders Show*); "Hey-yo" (Ed McMahon); "Hi-yo" (the Lone Ranger); "MMM-wahhhh" (Dinah Shore's vocalized good-bye kiss); "Nanoo nanoo" and "Shazrot" (Robin Williams's Mork); "Not," "Schwing," and "Way" (*Wayne's World*); "Oooh-oooh" (Officer Toody on *Car 54, Where Are You?*); "O-tay" (Eddie Murphy's Buckwheat); "Pow" (Ralph Kramden); "Schmock-schmock" (Steve Allen); "Well!" (Jack Benny); "Wocka wocka" (Fozzie Bear); "Woo" (the doglike call of the audience on *The Arsenio Hall Show* and *Total Request Live*); "Yabba dabba doo"

(Fred Flintstone); "Yadda yadda" (various characters on *Seinfeld*); "Yowza yowza" (Richie Cunningham on *Happy Days*, via Gig Young's character in *They Shoot Horses, Don't They?*, via bandleader Ben Bernie); and "Zoinks" (Shaggy on *Scooby Doo*).

I don't know about you, but I have to lie down for a minute. . . .

I'm back. As you can gather from the foregoing list, many interjections (the word comes from the Latin meaning "something thrown in") are, or seem to be, just one step away from nonsense words and barnyard noises. But they are very human. Specifically, they are essential to the way we talk—they convey attitude, emotion, and personality, which is why the most memorable characters are defined by them, not only in television but throughout popular culture. I give you Santa Claus's "Ho, ho, ho"; Charlie Brown's "Rats" and "Aaargh"; Curly's "Nyuk-nyuk" and "Soitenly!"; Annie Hall's "La-di-da"; and Rocky's "Yo!" More than any other word class, interjections are a part of *speech*.*

---

* You may be wondering why I didn't include some other famous taglines, like Steve Martin's "Excuuuuse me" or Phil Silvers's "Howaya." The answer is that they are more or less intelligible sentences. In the interest of narrowing down the category, I am counting as interjections only single words and those phrases (like "Hey now" and "Yabba dabba do") that have no syntactical standing.

Greek grammarians recognized no such word class, and their Roman successors added it, it has been surmised, only because they wanted to keep the number of parts of speech at eight and the Latin language has no articles. Early English grammarians weren't happy with this category, in any case. The ever-reliable eighteenth-century scold John Horne Tooke complained that

> the brutish inarticulate *Interjection*, which has nothing to do with speech, and is only the miserable refuge of the speechless, has been permitted, because beautiful and gaudy, to usurp a place among words. . . . The neighing of a horse, the lowing of a cow, the barking of a dog, the purring of a cat, sneezing, coughing, groaning, shrieking, and every other involuntary convulsion with oral sound, have almost as good a title to be called Parts of Speech, as Interjections have . . .
>
> Interjections are only employed when the suddenness or vehemence of some affection or passion returns men to their natural state; and makes them, for a moment forget the use of speech: or when, from some circumstance, the shortness of time will not permit them to exercise it.

No one has been quite able to do away with the interjection as a part of speech, but the enmity lingers.

Pullum and Huddleston allot it just five sentences in their 1,842-page *Cambridge Grammar*. David Crystal sniffs that it is "better treated as a type of sentence than as a word class." That comment points to part of the trouble: the words in this class throw aside the complexities and demands of syntax, which after all is what grammarians spend their careers studying. What makes it worse is that any word—indeed, any sound capable of human utterance—can be an interjection. Hello! Ha! Yes! Ciao! Stop! Idiot! Please! Sorry! Sit! You! Eraser! Potholder! Potrezebie!

For some words, the transition from marginal interjection to full-fledged member of the category is easy to trace. For example, the word *dude* originated in the 1880s as a slang noun meaning "dandy," probably derived from *duds*. About a half century later, African-American vernacular began using it (according to the *OED*) "approvingly, esp. . . . applied to a member of one's own circle or group"—that is, as a synonym for *cat*. In due time, white surfers appropriated it and began using it as a term of address. It spread to white youth culture generally, and the full use in this mode can be seen in films like *Bill and Ted's Excellent Adventure* and, of course, the seminal *Dude, Where's My Car?* The final transition for the word was to all-purpose interjection, described in Scott Kiesling's article "Dude" in *American*

Speech: "Dude may be used on its own as an exclamation, to express both positive and negative reactions (commonly with another exclamative, especially *whoa*)."*

One feature of many interjections helps explain the general disdain for the category. They are unseemly. *Echhhh* and many other interjections of disgust imitate or actually replicate the sound of human gagging. Then there are expressions of surprise or anger, and their many euphemistic cognates, which usually invoke sex or excretion or take God's name in vain. Thus we have *shit* and *sheesh, shoot,* and *shucks; fuck* and *fooey, fudge,* and *fiddlesticks; God* and *gosh, golly,* and *egad; goddamn* and *dagnabbit, doggonnit,* and the W. C. Fieldsian *God-frey Daniel;* and *Jesus Christ* and *jiminy cricket, jeepers,* and *gee whiz.* I'm not sure why an oath of *hell* was once considered profane, but it was, and thus begot *heck, Sam Hill,* and *h-e-double-hockey-sticks.* There are also such recondite and now-charming epithets as *zounds* (God's wounds), *'sblood* (God's blood), and *gadzooks* (God's hooks, that is, the nails used in Jesus's cross). The list goes on, including the common British and Irish *blimey,*

---

*Contrary to popular belief, Jeff Spicoli, the character played by Sean Penn in *Fast Times at Ridgemont High*, does not once utter the word *dude*.

which comes from the profane oath "God blind me!" and the well-known interjection of awe or astonishment *wow*, which originated as a Scottish version of *vow*, as in Robert Burns's 1789 line "And wow! he has an unco sleight O' cauk and keel." By the way, the first general use of *wow* cited by the *OED* is H. Rider Haggard's in 1892. It has been a popular word ever since, often ironically expanded into *wowee*, but took on special status in the countercultural movement of the 1960s. One of that movement's chief champions, Charles A. Reich, in maybe the goofiest passage in his book *The Greening of America*, praised:

> a childlike, breathless sense of wonder; this is the quality that Consciousness III supremely treasures, to which it gives its ultimate sign of reverence, vulnerability, and innocence, "Oh, wow!"

Interjections that express strong disagreement, intriguingly, tend to be references to the excrement of large animals or euphemisms thereof: *bullshit, baloney,* and *bushwah; horseshit, horsefeathers,* and *hogwash.* A pair of UK staples are the synonymous *balls* and *bollocks.* Inoffensive alternatives would include *applesauce, balderdash, humbug* (Scrooge's "Bah, humbug" is a nice double interjection), the effectively understated *please, poppycock*, and *pooh*, which Polonius uses to mock his daughter Ophelia: "Affection pooh! You speak like a green girl." The current youth favorite is *whatever*, which means, essentially, "What you just told me is so lame and stupid that it isn't even worth the energy it would take to dispute it." This can be extremely annoying, as any parent of a teenager can tell you. In June 2005, when the actor Russell Crowe complained to a hotel clerk in New York about the troubles he was having making a phone call to Australia, the clerk said, "Whatever," whereupon Crowe threw a telephone and a vase at him.

There are a lot of wholesome interjections, of course, most of which fall into a limited number of categories. Expressions of enthusiasm, like *yay*, *yippee*, and *hurray*, tend to be said more in comic strips than in real life. *Hello* and its synonyms, by contrast, are uttered millions of times a day. *Hey* is clearly a word with a past, what with all those *hey-diddle-diddles* and *hey-nonny-nonnies* in shepherds' songs. In the U.S., in the late nineteenth century, both it and *hi* became casual ways of greeting a friend or acquaintance; eventually, *hi* won out everywhere but in the American South, where *hey* persisted. To quote TV's favorite Marine again, "Tell him Gomer says, 'Hey.' " Auburn University, in Alabama, has since the 1940s observed an annual "Hey Day," when all faculty, students, and staff are supposed to greet each other with the word. *Hey* is also commonly used as an interjection of stressed surprise, as in, "Hey, what's the big idea?" Lately, *hey* has served another purpose, most egregiously among sports announcers and commentators, in statements like "When it comes to the postseason, hey, it's always defense that wins the day." Linguist Eric Hamp has commented that this *hey* contains "the rhetorically deliberate implication that what follows is obvious and therefore commands assent." *Hi*, meanwhile, has seen an uptick in recent years thanks to its popularity as an e-mail salutation; aside from starting off with pointed informality, it finesses the choice of addressing the recipient by first name or Mr./Ms./Miss.

Yo has followed its own twisting path—from the opening of the nautical call *yoho* (the verse "Fifteen men on a dead man's chest,/Yo-ho-ho and a bottle of rum" was included by Robert Louis Stevenson in his 1881 novel *Treasure Island* and put to music for a stage version twenty years later; years after that, *yoho* evolved into the familiar cozy greeting *yoo-hoo*), to World War II soldiers' way of saying "Present!," to the South Philadelphia greeting popularized by Rocky Balboa. One theory holds that this last *yo* derived from the Italian word *gualgione*, meaning "young man" and pronounced in dialect *gual-yoh*. The South Philly *yo* probably begat the hip-hop salutation of choice, which has been overdone to the point of absurdity by hip-hop wannabes. In a scene from the animated film *Shark Tales*, the fish with Martin Scorsese's voice sympathizes that Robert De Niro's shark can't snap its tail:

SCORSESE: It's OK. A lot of Great Whites can't do it, yo.

DE NIRO: Yo?

SCORSESE: Yo! Whassup?

DE NIRO: What's up with what?

SCORSESE: Yo yo yo! Yo yo yo. Yo yo yo, yo yo!

DE NIRO: Hey, you say "yo" one more time and I'm gonna yo you!

The *yo* in Scorsese's first line, or in such remarks as "I'm down with that, yo," has a distinct meaning, possessed by no other word I know. It's a sort of affirmative verbal punctuation mark, the way Mammy Yokum in *Li'l Abner* concluded any statement with "I has spoken!"

Probably the most popular use of interjections is as a way to express agreement, approval, or enthusiasm. In social discourse, people are always trying to find common ground, and interjections are an easy and convenient way to do so. Start with the simple *yes* (elongated into a catchphrase by basketball announcer Marv

Albert) and slang forms of it, including *yup*, *yessirree bob*, and *yeah*.* *Okay*, which probably deserves a chapter of this book to itself, originated, apparently in the 1830s, as a creatively spelled abbreviation for "all correct." *Amen*, *bingo*, *bravo*, *far out*, and the current hip-hop-derived *word* and *booyah* up the enthusiasm ante a little bit. Adjectives and adverbs come in and out of style as one-word affirmations, and most of them can be used either sincerely or ironically: *great*, *brilliant* (a favorite in the UK), *cool*, *solid*, *awesome*, *fantastic*, *fabulous*, *excellent*, *sweet*, *nice*, *really*, *absolutely*, *exactly*, *totally*. One favorite of my college buddies and mine does not appear in the dictionary. Our friend Ricos (the nickname of Lazaros Molho, now a distinguished economist with the World Bank), a native of Greece, used the word *ontos* to register agreement. When we asked him what it meant, he said it didn't have an exact translation, but it was an adverb form of a Greek verb meaning "to be" or "to exist." So we settled on "Existently!"

* *Yeah*, whose first OED citation dates from 1905, has a sort of gangster sound that belies how widely it's used in the United States. Perfectly fine in casual settings, it doesn't come off well in even moderately formal ones. One of the best pieces of advice I have ever gotten came from someone who had just heard me interviewed on the radio. "Don't say 'yeah' so much," he told me.

But interjections are not merely blunt instruments. You can see this by looking at a group of expressions that linguists have given various names, including fillers, stabilizers, and discourse markers. Some, like *so*, *well*, and *okay*, have lexical meanings in other contexts; others do not, including *mmm-hmmm*, *uh-huh*, and *huh*. Significant members of the group are the siblings *oh*, *o*, and *ah*, which were favorites of literary types for centuries, most popularly as a way to invoke strong emotion. Thus (to quote *Hamlet* again) "O, what a rogue and peasant slave am I!"; Stephen Foster's "Oh! Susanna"; the devastating last lines of Melville's "Bartleby the Scrivener"—"Ah, Bartleby! Ah, humanity!"; T. S. Eliot's "O o o o that Shakespeherean Rag"; and the tagline of *Saturday Night Live*'s Mr. Bill, "Ohhhh noooo."

Spoken *ohs* work differently from written ones. Linguist Deborah Schiffren, the reigning expert on these expressions and the author of the 1987 book *Discourse Markers*, has found that their general purpose is to "shift orientation to take account of just received information." Specifically, speakers can use *oh* to correct themselves, request clarification, correct someone else, make a request for elaboration, introduce a suddenly remembered question or remark, indicate ignorance of the just-given information, display recognition, or mark an intense reaction. When kicking off the answer to a question, the word can also be used as a way of neutralizing, or removing any tension from, the conversational moment. "How's your new girlfriend?" "Oh, not too bad." Like *huh*, *hmm*, and *ah*, *oh* can also be a way of saying *something* about a statement just made without committing oneself to a position; sometimes it edges into disappointment or disapproval. An old joke has it that the traditionally working-class institution of higher learning in Philadelphia should change its name from Temple U. to Temple O. because of the depressing (to alumni) familiarity of this exchange: "Where did you go to college?" "Temple." "Oh."

The frequent use of short expressions with no lexical meaning, to indicate or cover a pause or hesitation, tends to be a characteristic of certain social or linguistic groups, such as the upper-class British. Rudyard Kipling referred in 1913 to "life in smoking rooms / Seen through clouds of 'Ers' and 'Ums.'" More recently, those two words (as well as such variants as *uh* and *erm*) have been (over)used by would-be hip writers as mock vocalisms making sure the reader doesn't miss something supposedly surprising, notable, or humorous. Checking LexisNexis for references from the past week, I find the *Houston Chronicle* describing a group called Bellini as "certainly the only pop band today boasting a lineup with members from Austin, New

York City and, um, Sicily," and a *Los Angeles Times* columnist remarking, "In today's mixed cultural climate, a lot of exertion isn't required for seduction among the more, er, 'liberated' female." Ten years ago this was borderline clever. Now it's just lame.

Some interesting research has been done on what is known in the field as "minimal response": *uh-huh* and *okay* and the other things people say when someone else is speaking. Somewhat predictably, men tend to take the situation literally. That is, they say *uh-huh* if and only if they actually agree with what the person is saying. Women tend to send off a continual stream of these markers, as a means of support or "active listening." Men are a bit more stingy, Anna M. Fellegy writes. "Instead of appearing engaged throughout the conversation, men load up their responses at a specific syntactic unit." A recent entry in this category is the version of *all right*—pronounced "ah-ight"—that has come up in African-American vernacular. It can be a statement or a question, and a character in Spike Lee's film *Clockers* uses it as both: "Ah-ight, ah-ight?" There are lots of these one-word requests for confirmation or assent: *huh?*, *no?*, *right?*, the African-American *namsane?* ("know what I'm saying?"), the Canadian *eh?*, and the British working-class *innit?*, which is used in sentences like "You're going home tonight, innit?"

As the foregoing should suggest, interjections are by no means limited to conveying our bestial urges and reactions, as John Horne Tooke would have it. Some express some rather complex ideas. For example, *duh* (preferably pronounced in two syllables, the musical notes of which form a descending third) means, "You've stated something rather obvious," and *ka-ching* (ascending fourth), "That's a good idea. You might even make some money from it." The Yiddish *oy* expresses in just two letters a combination of aggravation and resignation that even a lengthy essay probably wouldn't do justice to. *Psst* means, roughly, "Come closer, without calling attention to yourself. I want to tell you something in confidence." *Psst*, incidentally, is an entirely consonantal syllable-word and is one of several interjections containing sounds that are found rarely, if at all, in the regular English phonetic inventory. Other complex interjections with unusual sounds, according to the online encyclopedia Wikipedia, are *ahem*, which contains a glottal stop; *shhh*, another consonantal syllable; *tsk-tsk*, which is made up entirely of clicks, an active part of regular speech in several African languages; and *whew*. Wikipedia reports that this expression of relief "starts with a bilabial fricative, a sound pronounced with a strong puff of air through the lips. This sound is a part of the native speech of Suki, a language of New Guinea."

That's another cool thing about interjections: they can carry you on all kinds of interesting cultural tours. Take the expression *hoo-hah*. I first encountered it as a kid in the pages of *Mad* magazine, where it was used as a kind of sardonic commentary, with a mock-Yiddish feel, on anything anybody said. I later learned that it was also the title of the first story in the first issue of the magazine. I forgot about it for years, until I saw the 1992 film *Scent of a Woman*. Frank Slade, the retired colonel played by Al Pacino, punctuates nearly every statement, or so I thought, with "Hoo-hah!" In another Marshall McLuhan moment, I wrote a letter to the author of the screenplay, Bo Goldman. He graciously wrote back, informing me that the term in the film wasn't "Hoo-hah" but "Hoo-ah." Goldman said he wasn't exactly sure why he put it in the script. He speculated that it may have come from the title of a Civil War musical he once wrote, *Hurrah, Boys, Hurrah*, the title of which was derived from a line in the song "The Battle Cry of Freedom": "the Union forever, hurrah, boys, hurrah."

(Goldman also said that the word was not as prominent in his screenplay as it became in the finished film. He explained that as shooting progressed, Pacino "became comfortable with the phrase and used it as an indescribable characterization of feeling satisfaction, excitement or minor triumph. . . . The main point is that Pacino, who is the most gifted actor I have ever worked with, when he finds a word or expression or phrase that gives him a handle on a character, will turn to it improvisatorially to make him comfortable at any given inarticulate moment in the drama, like an actor's security blanket.")

It turns out that *hoo-ah*, accent sometimes on the first syllable and sometimes on the second (and pronounced *oo-rah* by Marines), is a venerable military expression. There are differing theories on its origin. A plausible one has it as an abbreviation for "Heard, Understood, and Acknowledged." Rod Powers, writing for the About.com Web site, says some believe that it originated during the Vietnam War; U.S. soldiers adapted the Vietnamese word for "yes," which is pronounced *u-ah*. The expression has, in any case, become very popular in recent years. One can even walk into a convenience store and buy an energy bar called HooAH!, which was developed by the U.S. military. According to an e-mail from my friend Mark Bowden, the author of the nonfiction war narrative *Black Hawk Down*,

> For certain elite units *hoo-ah* has become a form
> of greeting, replacing the various forms of "hello"

and "goodbye." For two Rangers who meet as strangers, say, and discover in conversation that they belong or belonged to that unit, the revelation would almost certainly prompt an immediate "hoo-ah," as a higher, more meaningful form of greeting. On occasion, when a young soldier or veteran learns that I am the author of *Black Hawk Down*, he will look me in the eye and say, "hoo-ah," greeting me not just as an ordinary mortal, but as a brother.

The meaning of *hoo-ah* has apparently gone forth and multiplied. A humorous definition of the word, concocted by an anonymous wag and now found on military folks' Web sites throughout the Internet, gives a sense of the world of meaning a single interjection can contain. It states of *hoo-ah*:

Generally used when at a loss for words. Referring to or meaning anything and everything except "no." More specifically relates to: good copy, solid copy, roger, good or great; message received; understood; glad to meet you; welcome; I do not know, but will check on it; I haven't the vaguest idea; I am not listening; that is enough of your drivel; sit down; stop sniveling; you've got to be kidding; yes; yes sir;

affirmative; sure; ok; you got it; thank you; go to the next slide; you have taken the correct action; I don't know what that means, but am too embarrassed to ask for clarification; that is really neat, I want one too; and amen.

CHAPTER VI

N.

Generally speaking, things once they are named the name does not go on doing anything to them and so why write in nouns. Nouns are the name of anything and just naming names is alright when you want to call a roll but is it any good for anything else. To be sure in many places in Europe as in America they do like to call rolls. . . . Nouns as I say even by definition are completely not interesting.

—*Gertrude Stein*, "Lectures in America"

HAMLET: There are more things in Heaven and
   earth, Horatio,
Than are dreamt of in your philosophy.
—*Shakespeare*, Hamlet, *Act I, Scene 5*

Anyone, anywhere, anytime, who has made a list of the parts of speech has included on it nouns. They are the one kind of word without which communication is unimaginable. Their sheer inevitability makes defining them tricky. The elementary school definition most of us remember—a word that signifies a person, place, or thing—is more or less correct, if you accept that *beauty, running, health, entrance, confusion,* and similar words signify things. Grammarians and linguists prefer to define word classes by what they do. Nouns, unlike other parts of speech, can perform the following functions: occur after an article, determiner, or adjective; take a possessive *'s* and plural *s*; and act as the subject or direct object of a sentence. Not all nouns can do all these things. For example, in the sentence "Jeff is happy," *Jeff* is a noun but can't be preceded by a determiner or adjective. We normally talk about "the family car" rather than "the family's car," even though *family* is a noun and in this case the family can be said to possess the car. Adding one sheep to another sheep gives you two sheep, not two sheeps. And the subject of the sentence "Well-behaved campers will eat first" is not the word *campers,* but rather the noun phrase *well-behaved campers.*

Any word can be a noun, when it's referred to *as a word*—as when I might say to a student, "There are seventy-three *likes* and forty-one *awesomes* in your paper, Mr. Jones, and that's way too much." That's admittedly a parlor trick, but you can make virtually every adjective into a common noun by sticking a *the* in front of it. Doing that with the ten most frequently used adjectives—*the other*, *the good*, *the new*, *the old*, *the great*, *the high*, *the small*, *the different*, *the large*, and *the local*—produces something that sounds like a Bible verse. Adding *-ing* to a verb creates a noun ("Seeing is believing," "Parting is such sweet sorrow," "Breaking up is hard to do"). And common verbs are nouned with blinding frequency: the list starts with (having a) *say*, *make* (as in a brand of car), (giving it a) *go*, *look*, *use*, *find*, *work*, *need*, *feel*, *show*, *try*, *call*, *hold*, and *help*, and continues on for quite a long time indeed, up to recent and widely criticized noun coinages like *startup*, *redo*, and *get* (TV news talk for a highly sought-after interviewee).

Even leaving such altered words aside, English, like all other languages, contains vast multitudes of nouns—as it must, when you think of the urge of Adam and subsequent human beings to name all the things in heaven and earth. John Morse, managing director of Merriam-Webster, calculates that about 65 percent of the words in his company's unabridged dictionary are nouns. However, that underestimates the number of nouns in use, because the dictionary doesn't include person names, company names, brand names, band names, and other proper nouns, or technical or specialized terms—for ant species or chemical compounds or whatever—which are overwhelmingly nouns. What's more, the roster of nouns increases every day with new inventions, acronyms, car models, and company names; an exhaustive analysis of several new-word dictionaries found that nearly 78 percent of the entries were nouns. This was done in 1987, before the computer took off as an unimaginably rich noun source. Twenty years ago, who knew what the Internet was? The Internet begat the Web, which begat blogs, which begat bloggers, which begat the blogosphere—nouns all.

There would be even more nouns in the dictionary if English, instead of being mainly caseless and genderless, had eleven genders, like Swahili, or multiple cases instead of just two. In our language, the root form works for all purposes except the genitive, or possessive, which you generally get by merely appending an 's. Russian, by contrast, has six separate noun forms: nominative, genitive, dative, accusative, instrumental, and prepositional.

English is truly impressive, however, in the way it lets you construct nouns from verbs, adjectives, and other nouns; *blogger* and *blogosphere* are examples. All you have to do is add one of an assortment of suffixes: *-acy* (democracy), *-age* (patronage), *-al* (refusal), *-ama* (panorama), *-ana* (Americana), *-ance* (variance), *-ant* (deodorant), *-dom* (freedom), *-edge* (knowledge),

-ee (lessec), *-eer* (engineer), *-er* (painter), *-ery* (slavery),
-ese (Lebanese), *-ess* (laundress), *-ette* (launderette),
-fest (lovefest), *-ful* (basketful), *-hood* (motherhood),
-iac (maniac), *-ian* (Italian), *-ie* or *-y* (foodie, smoothy),
-ion (tension, operation), *-ism* (progressivism), *-ist* (ide-
alist), *-ite* (Israelite), *-itude* (decrepitude), *-ity* (stupid-
ity), *-ium* (tedium), *-let* (leaflet), *-ling* (earthling), *-man*
or *-woman* (Frenchman), *-mania* (Beatlemania), *-ment*
(government), *-ness* (happiness), *-o* (weirdo), *-or* (ven-
dor), *-ship* (stewardship), *-th* (length), and *-tude* (grati-
tude).

Some people go nuts with this kind of thing. The
eighteenth-century writer Horace Walpole coined the
word *serendipity*, meaning happy accident, based on
the title of the fairy tale *The Three Princes of Serendip*,
the heroes of which "were always making discoveries,
by accidents and sagacity, of things they were not in
quest of." Not content with that contribution, Walpole
also invented *gloomth*, *blueth*, and the last word of this
sentence from a 1753 letter: "I found my garden brown
and bare, but these rains have recovered the greenth."
A century later, John Ruskin coined *illth* as the opposite
of wealth.

At the present moment, *everybody* seems to be going
a bit nuts with noun creation. Journalists and bloggers
seem to believe that a sign of being ironic and hip is to

coin nouns with such suffixes as -fest (Google "bacon-fest" and behold what you find), -athon, -head (Dead-head, Parrothead, gearhead), -oid (the memorably named rock group Richard Hell and the Voidoids), -orama, and -palooza (a recent CD compilation of con-temporary performers paying tribute to retro music is called "Lounge-a-palooza"). I actually know the person responsible for another biggie. That's my former col-league Stephen Fried, who is credited by the OED with coining the word fashionista—meaning, roughly, some-one involved in or devoted to the world of fashion—in his 1992 book Gia. Stephen Frankenstein is more like it, considering the storm of -istas that has followed; one recent example is an article in the Daily Telegraph that calls supporters of David Beckham "Beckham-istas." Another trendy one is based on literati, a word that dates from 1621 and means influential literary types. The wrinkle here is that -ati endings seem to work only after words rhyming with or sounding like litter. That explains why it took until 1956 for someone (on the staff of Time magazine, not surprisingly) to come up with glitterati. Then came flitterati (from flit, meaning homosexual, and not listed in the OED but used in a Guardian article in 1987), digerati (1992), and bitterati (circa 2000).

The poppest of the ironic pop suffixes is -ster, which

had a venerable and fairly honorable beginning in such words as *huckster* (first use—1300), *trickster* (1711), *gangster* (1896), *roadster* (1908), and *hipster* (1941). The recent renaissance started even before Rob Schneider's Richmeister appeared on *Saturday Night Live*. I have on my bulletin board a yellowed clipping, dating from sometime in the early 1980s, of a letter published in the *Philadelphia Inquirer*, spurred by columnist Clark De Leon's revelation that his baby daughter Molly's nickname was "the Mollster." Reader Joan B. King wrote in to report that her own daughter

> Jodie, a reputed demon dragster in our little blue Escort, became known as "the Jodester of the Roadster" in her high school class. Soon this suffix mania struck our whole family. Sisters Jen, Julie and Joanie became "Jenster," "Julester," and "Joanster" and brother J.P. was dubbed "Jeepster." Of course, there's "Dadster" and "Momster."
>
> We were only sorry we had no hamster!

In the mid-1990s, a Massachusetts kid named Shawn Fanning was dubbed "the Napster" by his high school buddies because of his curly hair. Fanning went on to invent the world's first file-sharing sofware, called, naturally, Napster. Subsequently, Internet innovaters stuck

-ster at the end of the names of similar products: Grokster, Aimster (later Madster), Blubster, and Friend-ster. (This is similar to the process by which, ever since Watergate, journalists have dubbed all scandals *Something-gate*.) The world has now officially gone *ster*-crazy. At this point, the suffix is slapped on the end of virtually any word, even when the result makes no sense. A newspaper's movie plot summary: " 'Raising Helen': Kate Hudson is a New York scene-ster whose carefree lifestyle grinds to a halt when she finds herself responsible for her sister's adorable children."

Another unfortunate trend is the supersizing of nouns that already exist, apparently in the belief that the longer the word, the better. Pretentious haberdash-eries sell *shirtings* instead of *shirts*. I once read on a menu in Montana, "To prevent wastage, water will be served only on request." So what's wrong with *waste*? And in the B2B world, *signage* has pretty much taken over from *signs*, which sounds so . . . well, ordinary. I've learned that the *-age* phenomenon is more wide-ranging than I expected. It appears that a prime spreader of it (and many other novel usages) was the television series *Buffy the Vampire Slayer*. According to the book *Slayer Slang*, no fewer than fifty-five *age* coinages appeared in *Buffy* scripts, Web sites, and novelizations, including *agreeage*, *kissage*, and *weirdage*. You can find the official online journal of *Buffy* studies at www.slayage.com; on the home page, people who have made donations are thanked for their "supportage." But while *Buffy*'s writers may have popularized ironic *age*-age, they didn't invent it. I got into an e-mail discussion of the phenomenon with a couple of friends, one a bit under forty (I'll call him Bill), the other a bit over (Bob). Bob wrote, "*Spillage* was a word we used in college to denote inexpertly poured keg beer." Bill countered with *doobage*: n., marijuana, derived from *doobie*, slang for marijuana cigarette. Bob observed: "You might note that the difference between 'spillage' and 'doobage' pretty well sums up the difference between my college experience and Bill's."

Given their vast number, nouns are used more sparingly than you might expect: about 215 times in every thousand words, as recorded in the British National Corpus. And this category is strikingly absent among the most commonly used words in the language. The top noun, *time*, comes in at an unimpressive number sixty-six, followed by *people* (81), *way* (96), *years* (106), *year* (122), *government* (140), *day* (141), and *man* (142). Sadly but not surprisingly, *woman* lags far behind at 393.

When it comes to good writing, a fairly reliable principle is, the fewer nouns the better. Or, rather, simple nouns like *time*, *people*, *way*, *years*, *day*, *man*, and *woman* are unavoidable and fine: indeed, they're the pillars of the language. The problem comes with words that don't have such a precise and specific meaning. These words tend to be conjured up out of other words by *-acy*, *-age*, *-al*, and the other suffixes listed above, and are sometimes called nominalizations. Not surprisingly, the worst offender is academic prose. The authors of the book *Corpus Linguistics* examined some samples of this and found, for every million words of scholarly writing, forty-four thousand of them are formed from the suffixes *-tion/sion*, *-ness*, *-ment*, and *-ity*; fiction and speech both have about a quarter as many. The most common nominalizations included *movement*, *activity*, *information*, *relation*, and *equation*. A certain amount of this is okay, but it would be hard to argue that some academics don't take it too far. I quote from a scholarly book on my shelf (authors to remain nameless):

> For all these phenomena, the problem is to envisage a complex interaction between patterns and manifestations of patterns so that the logic of our statement does not force us to specify stages that we do

not need in our description or utterances for which
there can be no observational evidence.

But academics are hardly the only villains of the
piece; excessive nominalization is all over journalism,
corporate communication, political talk, and other
forms of public discourse. Fowler believed the words to
be most vigilantly avoided were ones ending in *-sion*
and *-tion*. He observed that "to count the *-ion* words in
what one has written, or, better, to cultivate an ear that
without special orders challenges them as they come, is
one of the simplest and most effective means of making
oneself less unreadable. . . . *Position* and *situation*, often
in combination, are special offenders." One could add
opportunity, *area*, *movement*, *activity*, *relationship*, *owner-
ship*, *information*, *indication*, and a few dozen others.
They pour out easily in writing (often preceded by the
flabby word *there* and a form of the verb *to be* and often
followed by a prepositional phrase and *another* nominalization), because they eliminate the need to decide and
precisely say who is doing or has done what to whom.
We say, "There are problems with your formulation of
the solution" because we're either too lazy or too scared
to say, simply and clearly, "You're wrong."

New York Times columnist David Brooks nailed

Harriet Miers, George W. Bush's star-crossed Supreme Court nominee, for the "vapid abstraction"—expressed with nouns—that marked the newsletter column she wrote as president of the Texas Bar Association. For example: "An organization must also implement programs to fulfill strategies established through its goals and missions. Methods for evaluation of these strategies are a necessity. With the framework of mission, goals, strategies, programs, and methods for evaluation in place, meaningful budgeting process can begin."

In addition to vapid abstraction, Miers's prose displays a common but little-observed writing glitch: poorly chosen subjects of clauses. It's probably impossible to escape serious prose trouble once you've saddled yourself with *organization*, *methods for evaluation*, or *meaningful budgeting process* as the subject of your sentence or clause; you're forced to reach for vague, passive, or unlikely verbs. A suggested guideline for writers: when you find you've written a sentence whose subject cannot be touched or visualized, think about revising.

Another noun problem is the piling up of them in phrases. Pairs like *grocery store*, *baseball player*, and *company town* are perfectly okay, but when three or more nouns in a row crowd up against each other, the result is not English but something turgid and limp. Yet, un-accountably, constructions like *consumer price index, income tax rate chart, fossil fuel product delivery system,* and *household bathroom shower head replacement unit* are proliferating. They're the kind of thing that make acronyms sound poetic.

You've probably gotten the point by now. Like Gertrude Stein, I'm not wild about nouns. And while I can't prevent them from dominating the dictionary, I certainly can—and am about to— terminate their participation in this book.

CHAPTER VII

Prep.

Pron. V. Adj. Adv. Art. Conj. Int. N.

What did you bring that book about Down Under that I didn't want to be read to out of up for?
—*Boy's question to his father, who's just climbed the stairs and walked into the lad's bedroom carrying a boring book about Australia*

As far as prepositions go, what we see is pretty much what we are going to get. That is, the English language rarely recruits any new prepositions, with the roster changing mainly when words fall out of it, as has happened to such golden oldies as *anent, aslant, athwart, atop, betwixt,* and *ere.* I say "rarely" because once in a while English appropriates a preposition from another language, such as French ("We're having dinner tonight *chez* the Bortkiewiczes"), legalese ("*Absent* any objections, I will eat this Devil Dog"), or African American Vernacular English ("If you don't be quiet, I'll hit you *upside* the head"). There's also a bit of wiggle room because sometimes the gerund form of verbs can create prepositions: *concerning, facing, including, re-garding*, etc. Anyway, other than these, the roster now stands at a bit more than forty: *about, above, across, af-ter, along, among, around, at, before, beside, between, be-yond, by, despite, down, during, for, from, in, inside, into, like, near, of, off, on, out, outside, over, since, through, throughout, till, to, toward, under, underneath, until, up, upon, with, within*, and *without*. You'll notice the list in-cludes some pairs, like *on* and *upon, under* and *under-neath, in* and *inside*, and *through* and *throughout*, that are close and sometimes identical in meaning.

As few and apparently simple as these words are, they are absolutely indispensable and include eight of the twenty most frequently used words in English: *of, to, in, for, with, on, by*, and *at*. The best place to find them is at the beginning of prepositional phrases. Some titular examples (which also give a sense of the preposition's versatility and piquancy): *Against Interpretation* (Sontag), "Behind Blue Eyes" (Townsend), *Beyond Good and Evil* (Nietzsche), "For Esmé, with Love and Squalor" (Salinger), *Inside Daisy Clover* (Mulligan), *Of a Fire on the Moon* (Mailer), "Over the Rainbow" (Arlen-Harburg), *Through a Glass Darkly* (Bergman), "To a Skylark" (Keats), and *Under the Volcano* (Lowry).

Despite its popularity, this part of speech is hard to

get a handle on. Samuel Johnson's dictionary of 1755 gave forty-two meanings for *for*, and *Webster's Unabridged* has thirty-one separate ones for *on*. It's easy to recognize that prepositions delineate relationships, but fixing a precise common definition for them is more slippery, as John Horne Tooke recognized in 1793:

> The Grammarian says, it is none of his business, but that it belongs to the philosopher: and for that reason only he omits giving an account of them. While the Philosopher avails himself of his dignity; and, when he meets with a stubborn disdain which he cannot unravel (*and only then*), disdains to be employed about *Words*: although they are the necessary channel through which his most precious liquors must flow.

Tooke thought prepositions were a necessary evil: "I will venture to lay it down as a rule, that, of different languages, the least corrupt will have the fewest Prepositions." However, the anonymous author of an eighteenth-century book called *The English Accidence* gave preps. their props: "As the members of the body are knit together by *nerves*, *tendons*, and *ligaments*, without which they would be useless and no way serviceable either to themselves or to one another; so, prepositions are the *nerves* and *ligaments* of all discourse." And in *Connectives of English Speech*, published in 1904, James Fernold opined that without prepositions and other connectives, "all speech would be made up of brief, isolated and fragmented statements. The movement of thought would be constantly and abruptly broken. Much would need to be guessed at; much would, after all, be doubtful or obscure; while the mental difficulty involved in following such statements would render them practically useless."

Be that as it may, a definition would still be nice. In *The Concise Oxford Companion to the English Language*, Tom McArthur offers a helpful summary of the sorts of things prepositions concern:

(1) Space and time, many being used for both: *at* in *They met at Heathrow Airport at six o'clock*. (2) Cause and purpose: *for* in *She did it for reasons of her own*. (3) Agent and instrument: *by* in *work done by an assistant*; *with* in *opened with a knife*. (4) The versatile *of*: possessive (*a friend of mine, the lid of the box*); assigning origin (*of royal descent*); indicating creation (*the works of Shakespeare*); referring to depiction (*a picture of Loch Fyne in winter*); indicating a subject of

conversation (*telling them of his travels*); stating
source and manufacture (*made of cotton*).

Sometimes you see a preposition that isn't followed
by a noun. This can be because the word is acting not
as a preposition but as an adverb ("We went *outside*";
"Profits are going *up*") or because it is part of a verb-
preposition combination, known as a "phrasal verb,"
that has a meaning notably different from what the definitions of the two words in themselves would suggest:
for example, "Pretty soon the Eagles will kick *off*," or
"When are you coming *in*?" The words phrasal verbs
usually conclude with—*off, in, up, out, down*—are interesting in that they can serve as either adverbs ("Love
Walked In") or prepositions ("In My Life"). That has
led some grammarians to consider these words as a separate part of speech, known as particles.

"Pretty soon the Eagles will kick off" would appear
to violate one of the all-time great grammatical shibbo-
leths: that when writing a sentence or clause, you must
not commit the crime I'm about to perpetrate, and
make a preposition the last word you put in. This notion apparently originated with the poet John Dryden,
who in a 1672 work quoted Ben Jonson's line "The
bodies that these souls were frighted from" and com-

mented: "The Preposition at the end of a sentence; a common fault with him, and which I have but lately observ'd in my own writings." Probably, Dryden based his stand on two foundations. First, prepositions in Latin never appear at the end of a sentence, not surprising since *praepositio* is Latin for something that "comes before." Second, a principle of composition that's as valid in the twenty-first century as it was in the seventeenth holds that, whenever possible, sentences should end strongly—and prepositions, as necessary as they undeniably are, are usually more of a whimper than a bang.

Whatever its origin, the ban found favor with prescriptivists through the centuries, including Edward Gibbon; John Ruskin, who in an entire book (*Seven Lamps*) concluded a sentence with a preposition precisely one time; Lily Tomlin's officious Ernestine the telephone operator, who asked, "Is this the party to whom I am speaking?"; and my mother-in-law, Marge Simeone, who is prone to saying things like "In which car are we going?" Not that it matters to Marge (who is also the only person I know who observes the traditional distinction between *shall* and *will*), but the myth was always a bit suspect. It was blown out of the water by Fowler, who wrote in *A Dictionary of Modern English Usage*, "Those who lay down

the universal principle that final prepositions are 'inelegant' are unconsciously trying to deprive the English language of a valuable idiomatic resource, which has been
used freely by all our greatest writers except those whose
instinct for English idiom has been overpowered by no-
tions of correctness derived from Latin standards." Fowler
then gave twenty-four examples of the "rule" being broken by such writers as Chaucer, Spenser, Milton, Pepys,
Swift, Defoe, Burke, Kipling, and the authors of the King
James Bible. He did not quote the line from *The Tempest*
"We are such stuff as dreams are made on," but that's a
good example of the problem with the rule. To transpose
an ultimate preposition, one usually has to lose rhythm
and add words, often including that lame relative pronoun *which*. Thus the Bard would have had to amend
Prospero's line to read, "We are such stuff on which
dreams are made," and nobody, not even Dryden, could
consider that an improvement.* Similarly, who can
imagine Edwin Starr singing, "War—for what is it
good?"? When the preposition occurs in a phrasal verb,
the transposition task can be close to impossible. To "fix"
a phrasal-verb-concluding sentence like "I'm turning in,"

---

* The line is often misquoted to conclude "as dreams are made
of," and in fact it appears on the Internet this way seventy-one
times, compared to sixty-three with the correct *on*.

you'd have to come up with something like "Turning in I am," which not even Yoda from *Star Wars* could say with a straight face.

To anyone still unconvinced, I offer two small anecdotes, in reverse order of familiarity.

1. Winston Churchill, when corrected for violating this rule, supposedly replied, "That is the sort of nonsense up with which I will not put."

2. A guy from South Philadelphia, on vacation in London, asks a bowler-hatted gent, "Where's the subway at?" The Londoner replies, "Don't you Yanks realize that it's poor English to end a sentence with a preposition?" To which the South Philly guy says, "Okay, where's the subway at, *asshole?*"

Stop me if you've heard this one, but I can't resist one more joke. Sent to prison as a first-time offender, an English student was told by a longtime inmate that if he made amorous advances to the warden's wife, she would get him released quickly. "But I can't do that," he protested. "It's wrong to end a sentence with a proposition." (Thank you, joe-ks.com!)

Incidentally, my mother-in-law regularly utters one particular preposition-ending sentence. The sentence is

"Are you coming with?"—meaning, "Are you coming with me?" I thought this was a charming idiosyncrasy until I read an article in *American Speech* that identified the "elliptical *with*" as an idiom found in Chicago, which happens to be Marge's hometown. I have since learned of a distinguished Windy City eating establishment called Harold's Chicken Shack, in which, I am told, one may order one of two things: "chicken" or "chicken *with*" (i.e., with hot sauce).

I have been busting on Dryden and his heirs, but they're perfectly correct when they say that prepositions can be problematic. One can search long and hard in dictionaries of memorable quotations and still unearth very few where this word class is a key element. There's Lincoln's "Of the people, by the people, for the people," of course, and, from *The Book of Common Prayer*, "Through Christ, and with Christ, and in Christ, all honor and glory are yours." A great deal more obscure is Byron's description of a "little isle":

> . . . *in it there were three tall trees,*
> *And o'er it blew the mountain breeze,*
> *And by it there were waters flowing,*
> *And on it there were young flowers growing.*
>   *Of gentle breath and hue.*

Beyond that, I'd have to invoke the old cigarette jingle that proclaimed, "Over, under, around, and through, Pall Mall carries the flavor to you," and Timothy Leary's immortal series of phrasal verbs: "Turn on, tune in, drop out."

Prepositions are not exactly the most muscular part of speech. And, because they are doubled in some expressions—*in accordance with, by means of, in addition to, get in on*, and so forth—they have the capability of piling up in truly frightening numbers. Thus the little boy's questions reproduced at the beginning of this chapter. Prepositions are also prone to particular solecisms and infelicities. The main problem is figuring out which one to use; as often as not, the choice of the preposition in an idiomatic expression makes no sense at all. Why should something offered free of charge be *on*, rather than *in, of, by, from*, or *for* the house? No reason at all, other than custom. I pity the person learning English who has to figure out and remember the difference between blame *on* and blame *for*. Preposition choice probably beats out irregular verbs as the number one booby trap for newcomers to the language. On an Italian vacation just ended, I stayed in a hotel that (the brochure announces) "provides of a pleasant breakfast room with a quality buffet service and of a typical terrace for your relax." Native speakers have a problem

with this, too. In an article for the late, lamented journal *Verbatim*, Barbara DuBois offered a few hundred examples of misused prepositions, culminating in this
rousing conclusion:

> Don't let people express a *predilection with*; don't let
> them *look upon you for advice*; don't let them have an
> *attitude over the project* or *unpack the contents on this
> package*. Complain when the sports reporter asks the
> famous athlete whether he is *a target by the police*.
> Above all, don't let *rising costs stand in your way from
> achieving your goal*, even if life does *reek with politics* and
> even if the earth does become *barren from vegetation*.

Sometimes, of course, accepted usage changes. For
some decades, the venerable phrase *enamored of* has
been challenged by *enamored with* (probably because of
the latter's similarity to *in love with*). The challenger
now seems poised to take control. A Yahoo search
yields 1.22 million hits for *enamored with* (including a
quotation by Tom Cruise about his feelings vis-à-vis
Katie Holmes) and 1.2 million for *enamored of*.

Another peril is prepositional redundancy, as in Paul
McCartney's line from "Live and Let Die," named in several online bulletin boards as the worst song lyric of all
time: "This ever-changing world in which we live in." I

mentioned earlier the usefulness of prepositions in titles, but they can also be dismayingly portentous (*From Here to Eternity*, *Of Human Bondage*) and something of a crutch. A colleague who had previously been a newspaper editor once pointed out to me the usefulness of *beyond* when one is stuck for a headline for a lifestyle article. A piece about trends in Japanese food—"Beyond Sushi"; about backyard games—"Beyond Badminton"; about choosing annual plants—"Beyond Geraniums." The formula is endlessly adaptable, and endlessly adapted it has been. I had that conversation more than twenty years ago, and rarely has a week passed since in which I haven't seen a "Beyond" headline. *Around*, meanwhile, is a psychobabble favorite: "He has issues around death."

For some reason, prepositions are frequently used to convey a sense of self-importance. You know you're in for a high-minded snorer when a movie's credits announce that it's based "upon" (rather than plain old "on") some novel. Pomposity joins with passive aggression when receptionists inquire, "What is this regarding?" For some reason, my students are attached to the word *amongst*, which means the same as *among* except that it has two extra letters and makes you sound like a character out of P. G. Wodehouse. As yet I have not received a paper with the word *whilst*, but the day is young.

I picked up my morning newspaper today to read about

construction plans for something called The Shoppes at Essington. What it is is a strip mall on Essington Avenue, a gritty street in Southwest Philadelphia. Even more than the capitalized "The" and the misspelled "Shoppes," the *at* is a poignant try at adding cachet. And people who say, "I was *at* [instead of just *went to*] Harvard" or "He works *on* [instead of *for*] the *Washington Post*" are engaged in preening-by-preposition. The baseball team named the Los Angeles Angels *of* Anaheim is a little pretentious, but mostly just weird.

Prepositions foster sins of omission as well as commission. I have no objection to native Yiddish speakers of a certain age asking, "Why don't you have a nice glass tea?" or with Britishers saying they will meet me at "half nine" or "a week Sunday." But for some reason, when I hear someone say "a couple hours" or "a high-class type person," I feel like screaming, "ARE YOU SO FREAKING BUSY YOU DON'T HAVE TIME TO SAY A TWO-LETTER WORD LIKE 'OF'?" *Of* ellipsis seems to be spreading, as in a published sentence I came across recently for which there is no excuse: "I'm an adult with plenty knowledge of my own." On the other hand, many people like to stick in a not strictly necessary *of*, as in "He looked out of the window," Huck Finn's remark "I'd borrow two or three dollars off of the judge," and "It's not that big of a deal."

The last construction has become sadly unavoidable.

I imagine that it originated as an echo of phrases like "a prince of a fellow" or "not that much of a problem," which are grammatically unimpeachable because *prince* is a noun and *much* used that way is a pronoun. But *big* and *good* are adjectives and so don't require an *of*. Following them with one is certainly not a threat to the republic, but I do get a fingernails-on-the-blackboard reaction when the noun that follows is a collective one, as in the quote uttered by many a losing baseball pitcher: "I didn't have that good of stuff today."

The preposition *about* is often hauled in to denote something akin to essential meaning, as in David Mamet's statement "Poker is about money." The first person who used it this way was fairly clever; the legions of others, not so. The same with the various permutations. It's fine that Lance Armstrong called his book *It's Not About the Bike*, but not that Wyatt Webb and Brandi Chastain called theirs *It's Not About the Horse* and *It's Not About the Bra*. Ditto "I'm about . . ." or "I'm all about . . . ," which adds the sin of solipsism to that of cliché mongering. Lines like "It's not about you" or "It's not about the money anymore" or "This is about us" have become a staple, perhaps *the* staple, of bad movies. Perhaps one of those famous screenwriting courses teaches you to stick one of them in when there's a lull in the action. On the other hand, another screenwriting cliché elides *about* and makes *to talk* into a transitive verb, as in the title of a 1992 film, *We're Talking Serious Money*.

It's a fact universally acknowledged that good stylists are sparing with prepositions. Bryan Garner, in *Modern American Usage*, counsels writers to determine their own "preposition quotient"; he says that one preposition in every four words is common in flabby prose, but that in better writing it's more like one in ten or fifteen. I put this to the test. Not surprisingly, legal, bureaucratic, official, and technical language is preposition-heavy. The Pledge of Allegiance's thirty-one words contain eight prepositions ("*to* the Republic, *for* which it stands . . .")—a little more than one in four. The ratio is almost exactly one in five in this passage from the manual for my TiVo (which I do *not* use to TiVo television programs):

> Connect the Coaxial RF cable coming *out of* the wall *to* the In socket *on* the splitter. Connect a Coaxial RF cable *from* one Out socket *on* the splitter *to* the Antenna/Cable RF In jack *on* the DVR. Connect another Coaxial RF cable *from* a second Out socket *on* the splitter *to* the Antenna In jack *on* your TV. (See the User's Guide *for* more information *on* this setup.)

When it comes to words that are meant to be read, many writers would do well to heed Garner's advice.

Certainly this passage from the *Philadelphia Inquirer* sports section truly suffers by virtue of its overstuffed preposition quotient:

> *In* the midst *of* a pennant race, the Phillies are 17–2 *over* the last month, which is a far cry *from* the 17-game stretch that began *in* late May and saw them go 15–2 and bat .318 *against* the likes *of* San Francisco, Florida, Atlanta, Arizona, Texas and Milwaukee *en* route *to* putting themselves *into* playoff contention *after* a subpar start.

But the goal of one preposition in fifteen words seems a trifle ambitious. I crunched the numbers in passages from some texts on hand: a John Updike essay, Nabokov's *Speak, Memory*, Lewis Carroll's *Through the Looking Glass*, and a front-page article from the *New York Times*. In each case, prepositions accounted for a remarkably consistent 9 to 11 percent of the total word count, and it would seem that a writer would do fine to stay in this territory.

Garner offers an eminently sensible five-point plan for cutting down on your prepositions. First, you can sometimes simply delete a prepositional phrase without losing meaning: "senior vice president of the corporation" can become "senior vice president." Second, uncover "buried verbs"—changing, for example, "is in violation of" to "violates" or "is the owner of" to "owns." (This also gets rid of "to be" verbs and flabby nouns, always a plus.) Third, replace a prepositional phrase with an adverb: "she did it stylishly" instead of "she did it with style." Fourth, replace *of* ("the convenience of the reader") with a possessive ("the reader's convenience"). Fifth, change from passive to active verbs, so that "the ball was hit by Jane" becomes "Jane hit the ball."

True, true, true. Yet as with other maligned parts of speech, prepositions' admitted gaucheries can obscure their charms. A commonplace of stylistic prescriptivism is a riff on allegedly superfluous preposition addition. Ernest Gowers, for example, claims that the phrasal verbs *meet up with*, *visit with*, *lose out*, *lose out on*, *close down*, *face up to*, *try out*, *miss out on*, *rest up*, and *head up* would all mean the same thing minus the preposition or prepositions with which they conclude. One could add to the list *divide up*, *up until*, *hurry up*, *continue on*, *on top of*, and many other expressions. I would defend most of them. There is such a thing as salutarily emphatic redundancy, which is why the slogan "Raid Kills Bugs Dead" (written by the Beat poet Lew Welch in a stint as an adman) is so memorable; in these phrases, the added preposition or short adverb usually adds an element of emphasis, intensity, or completion. "I'm going to clean" is not the same as "I'm going to clean up." *Merriam-Webster's Dictionary of English Usage* nails the normally scrupulous Bill Bryson for doing, in his book *The Mother Tongue*, the very thing he's criticizing. Bryson writes, "In a sentence such as 'He climbed up the ladder,' the *up* does nothing but take up space." Why not just "take space," Bill?

Similarly, any ten-year-old who pays attention in English class knows that the sentence "Where are you at?" is "incorrect"; the *at* is implied in the *where*. But it's an awfully effective redundancy. In New Orleans, "Where y'at?" (i.e., "Where are you at?") is such a ubiquitous greeting that *yat* has become a term both for the local lingo and for a native New Orleanian. African-American slang gave the *where-at* combo a more generalized, existential meaning. This was appropriated by the hippies, who were prone, as the writer Cyra McFadden ingeniously pointed out, to use spatial pronouns as psychological descriptors: "I can get *behind* that," "I see where you're coming *from*," "Are you *down* with that?," "He's *into* ceramics," "Anybody *up* for a veggie burger?"

As a matter of fact, prepositions shine as catalysts for the regeneration of the language. In the preface to his dictionary of 1755, Dr. Johnson wrote:

There is another kind of composition more frequent in our language than perhaps in any other, from which arises to foreigners the greatest difficulty. We modify the signification of many verbs by a particle subjoined; as to *come off*, to escape by a fetch; to *fall on*, to attack; to *break off*, to stop abruptly; to *bear out*, to justify; to *fall in*, to comply; to *give over*, to cease; to *set off*, to embellish; to *set in*, to begin a continual tenour; to *set out*, to begin a course or journey; to *take off*, to copy; with innumerable expressions of the same kind, of which some appear wildly irregular, be-ing so far distant from the sense of the simple words, that no sagacity will be able to trace the steps by which they arrived at the present use.

Some of Johnson's examples are no longer current, and even some definitions are obscure to us (*fetch*: dodge, trick, or stratagem; *tenour*: alternate spelling of "tenure"). But the phenomenon he was talking about is still going on, and still baffling and maddening people trying to learn the language. Very long books have been filled with lists of thousands and thousands of phrasal verbs. You can appreciate the vastness if you consider just some of those that start with a single verb. Check out the difference in meaning, moving from innocent to pretty much the op-posite, in these phrasals: *sleep over*, *sleep through*, *sleep on (it)*, *sleep in*, *sleep off*, *sleep with*, *sleep around*. Quite often phrasal verbs turn into hyphenated or single-word nouns: e.g., *takeoff* (a parody or the start of a rocket's flight), *takeout* (food carried away from a restaurant), *takeover* (one business assuming control of another), *takedown* (a successful wrestling move), and *take-away* (current corporate jargon for the lessons learned from a meeting or seminar). Prepositions can also fruitfully switch categories, for example, into adjectives, as in the currently popular *after party* or the sentence "I gained so much weight I looked like a before photo."

You're getting the idea, I hope, that slang absolutely depends on prepositions. I could fill the rest of this book giving examples, but I will confine myself to the arena that I (to my mild embarrassment) know best: sports. Since it's the national pastime, let's take a prepositional tour of baseball. The batter steps *up* to the plate. The pitcher shakes *off* a sign, then looks *off* a base runner. First pitch: *inside*. Second one: *on* the corner. The third is right *over* the plate—*down* the middle. If the batter gets *under* the pitch, he will pop *up*, after which the shortstop will call the second baseman *off* and haul *in* a can *of* corn. If the hitter gets *on* top *of* it, he will probably hit it *in* the dirt and ground *out*. But if he gets good wood *on* it, he could well hit it *down* the line or *in* the gap. He may even knock it *over* the fence, at which point the announcer will say, "It's *out of* here." It may even be a walk-*off* home run. On the other hand, if the pitcher is *in* the groove, he could pitch a shut-*out*. And you could look it *up*.

With the hallowed half dozen of *up*, *down*, *in*, *out*, *on*, and *off*, a seemingly infinite number of expressions can be generated. *Psych up*, *get down*, *give in*, *freak out*, *right on*, and *bug off* are merely arbitrary starting points, after which one could move into altered parts of speech: all six can be used as adjectives, and all but *on* and *in* as pungent verbs. (*Up* = raise; *down* = swallow quickly, or, in sports, defeat; *out* = expose as a homosexual; *off* = murder.)

Up is probably the most fertile particle. Not only does it intensify verbs, but it can be combined with various other parts of speech to *create* verbs. A character on the always linguistically interesting television series *Buffy the Vampire Slayer* once remarked, "Gee, can you vague that up for me?"; a current ad campaign for the Best Buy electronics chain invites customers to "Plus up your experience with our pros"; and the pitcher Satchel Paige advised, "Avoid fried meats which angry up the blood." *Hook up* is a ubiquitous term on college campuses meaning to have a romantic encounter; the hyphenated form can refer either to the experience or the partner. The biggest British press scandal of all time erupted when the

Blair government was accused of trying to "sex up" find-
ings of weapons of mass destruction in Iraq. That re-
minds me of the British noun *run-up*, meaning the period
of time leading up to a certain event, which has been enthusiastically taken up by the American press, and *mash-
up*, a blend of two songs or albums into a single musical
work. Adjectives formed by the *verb past tense + up* combination are a current favorite, notably in the expression
"That's messed up," used to indicate a wide range of dis-
pleasure, disapproval, or regret. (*Messed up* is, of course, a
euphemism for *fucked up*.)

The histories of the expressions *mobbed up* and
lawyered up are interesting to compare. The former, indicating an unspecified but extensive connection to or-
ganized crime, is first cited by the *OED* in the 1963
Senate testimony of Mafia informant Joseph Valachi.
But it has taken off in recent years, presumably inspired
by *Goodfellas*, *The Sopranos*, and other mob narratives.
Lawyered up, meaning that a criminal suspect is in pos-
session of legal counsel, on the other hand, appears to
have been originated by the writers of the TV program
NYPD Blue, which went on the air in 1993. By 1997,
life was imitating art, as a spokesman for the St. Peters-
burg, Florida, sheriff's office told the *St. Petersburg
Times* that a suspect was "lawyered up and not talking."
Today the phrase is a commonplace.

Certain national, ethnic, regional, and occupational subcultures appear to have preferences for particular prepositional uses. I'm awestruck by the myriad ways African American Vernacular English uses the word *on*. James Brown sang "Get on the Good Foot," and two of Marvin Gaye's greatest songs were "Let's Get It On" and "What's Going On." The meaning of the last phrase has in recent years expanded from noncommittal description to valorization: "The Pistons had it going *on* last night." "It's on me" means that the speaker is accepting responsibility or blame. Like *up*, *on* can be added to certain verbs as an intensifier: "I'm digging on you" and, as receiver Terrell Owens modestly said in explaining why he didn't mind criticism, "People hated on Jesus." To *bust on* a person is to insult him or her. *On the downlow* is a secret homosexual life, and kids who are grounded or whose privileges are taken away are *on punishment*. I haven't been able to figure out if the transitive verb *hit on*, meaning to aggressively flirt, has an African American origin; I would guess yes. The 1930s jazz slang *in the groove* begat the intransitive verb *groove* (and the adjective *groovy*), which developed into the transitive verb *groove on*, meaning to intensely enjoy something. This in turn presumably combined with the venerable expression "Get a move on" to produce the 1960s phrase "Get your groove on," which became the template for such variations as "Get your freak on" (variously used to connote dancing, drugs, and sex), "Get your learn on," and "Get your laugh on." These are still current as far as I can tell, but they may not be for long, now that the mainstream culture has taken notice. On the TV comedy *Scrubs*, the medical resident Todd, a wannabe African-American, is mocked for saying he's going to "get his grub on" rather than just plain eat, and in an episode of *The O.C.*, a character who's in trouble for shady business practices is told, "It's time to get your Martha Stewart on." Even worse, Lay's Potato Chips has adopted the slogan "Get your smile on."

The glamour preposition of the last two decades, without question, is not a word but a symbol—specifically, the @ sign. It is the one common component of every e-mail address on earth, and it has generated an abundance of cute nicknames. According to the Web site Webopedia, in Czech it is referred to as "rollmop" or "pickled herring," in Dutch as "monkey's tail," in French as "little snail," in Greek as "little duck," in Hebrew as "strudel," in Swedish as "*a* with an elephant's trunk," and in Thai as "the wiggling wormlike character."

Of course, @ predates e-mail. Giorgio Stabile, a professor of the history of science at La Sapienza University in Italy, recently found a sixteenth-century letter that used the symbol to represent an amphora, a clay vessel used to carry grain and wine. It eventually became a commonly understood symbol meaning "at the price of"—so common that it was included on the first typewriter keyboard in the late 1800s.

Fast-forward a hundred years or so, to 1972. Ray Tomlinson, an engineer at the Cambridge, Massachusetts, consulting firm of Bolt, Beranek, and Newman, was working on a project in which staff members at the company would transfer files and send messages among a series of networked computers around the country: in other words, e-mail. To indicate where the sender was "at," Tomlinson decided to use the @ sign to precede the name of the host computer.

In an interview not long ago, he said the decision was pretty much a no-brainer:

"If you look at the keyboard, there really aren't a whole lot of choices. The one that really stands out is the at sign, because it indicates where a user might be. It's the only preposition on the keyboard."

CHAPTER VIII

Pron. V. Adj.
Adv. Art. Conj.
Int. N. Prep.

Is me her was you dreamed before? Was then
she him you us since knew? Am all them and
the same now me?

—*James Joyce*, Ulysses

When people get upset over language, more often than
not the crux of the problem is a pronoun. This makes
sense. Pronouns are words used in place of a noun or
noun phrase, and in that act of substitution you can
find a world of attitudes and belief.

Consider: "The typical student in the program takes
about six years to complete their coursework." Eighty-
two percent of the American Heritage Dictionary Usage Panel declared the *their* rendered this sentence
unacceptable. The judgment is certainly in keeping
with traditional grammar. *Student* is singular, so the possessive pronoun later in the sentence shouldn't be the
plural *their*, but rather the singular . . . what? Ah, their's
the rub. It turns out that this "traditional grammar" is

pretty new. Before the eighteenth century, writers and speakers typically referred to an indefinite subject— *everyone, anyone, a person,* or *the typical student*—with a *they, their,* or *them,* sometimes known as the "epicene pronoun." Examples are plentiful. Shakespeare's *Much Ado About Nothing*: "God send every one their heart's desire!" The King James translation of the Bible: "in lowliness of mind let each esteem others better than themselves." Fielding's *Tom Jones*: "Every Body fell a laughing, as how could they help it."

However, the fervent eighteenth- and early-nineteenth-century grammarians collectively decided a) that indefinite subjects were singular, and b) that the appropriate pronoun for such subjects was the "masculine generic," that is, *he, him,* and *his.* a) is defensible; the words *one, body, person,* and *student* are indeed singular nouns, after all. But b) is not. *They* had been doing effective double duty for centuries as singular and plural (much like *you*), but even if it were to be changed, why on earth should the masculine be chosen as the generic? Even a couple of hundred years ago, apparently, some people were asking themselves this question, for the English Parliament felt compelled in 1850 to pass a law banning the official use of the expression *he or she* in favor of the generic *he.* This is the basis of

the grammar that we, and our parents, and our grand-
parents, and at least 82 percent of the American Heritage Dictionary Usage Panel, all learned in school. It
led to the publication of such impossible but "correct"
sentences as "No person shall be forced to have an
abortion against his will" and "Man, being a mammal,
breast-feeds his young."

But the epicene pronoun secretly thrived. In the
years of its proscription, most people apparently continued to use it in speech, and a surprising number did so
in writing as well. Linguist Henry Churchyard has com-
piled on his Web site eighty-seven instances of the singular *they*, *their*, or *them* in the works of Jane Austen
alone, and additional nineteenth- and twentieth-
century examples are plentiful. Whitman: "Everybody
delights us, and we them." Oscar Wilde: "Experience is
the name everybody gives to their mistakes." Gertrude
Stein: "It is very hard telling from any incident in any
one's living what kind of being they have in them."
Sting: "If you love someone, set them free." Concur-
rently, as Dennis Baron reported in a 1981 article in
American Speech, an impressive variety of genderless,
singular alternatives was put forward. The earliest he
found was *ne*, from about 1850, the same year that Parliament outlawed *he or she*. Coincidence? Maybe. It was

followed, Baron reports, by *en*, *thon*, *le*, *ip*, *ir*, *ons*, *e*, *hizer*, *he'er*, *hesh*, *hes*, *se*, *hse*, *co*, *ve*, *tey*, *fm*, *ze*, *hiser*, *himer*, *es*, *ha*, *himorher*, *na*, *s/he*, *em*, *ae*, and *hir*. Today, one sees *s/he* in academic and bureaucratic prose, but of the others, the only one to have had even a smidgen of success is *thon*, a blend of *that one* coined by lawyer and composer Charles Crozat Converse in 1884. (Among Crozat's credits was the hymn "What a Friend We Have in Jesus.") *Thon* had its adherents, including the famed chiropractor D. D. Palmer, who wrote that the best way to get a patient to relax was to "place thon's arms beside and parallel to the body." The word was included in dictionaries as late as 1964 but is now as archaic as *anent*. The surprising thing is that it had as much success as it did: new nouns, verbs, adjectives, adverbs, and interjections enter the language all the time, but it is nearly impossible to create a new pronoun, preposition, conjunction, or article (known collectively as the grammatical parts of speech).

Since the feminist movement of the 1970s, distaste for the generic masculine has intensified; today, using it is a marker of retrograde chauvinism. But none of the alternatives is really satisfactory. *He or she* sounds nerdy, *s/he* isn't English, using the generic feminine (as some

academics and many feminists do) is protesting too
much, and alternating *he* and *she* is just plain confusing.
I predict, therefore, that *they* will carry the day. In addition to avoiding the awkwardness or self-congratulation
of other usages, it can provide a useful sense of gender
indeterminacy: "I was talking to someone at a bar, and
they gave me their phone number." A sign of the tide
turning is that in the last decade, the epicene *they* has
appeared more and more in journalistic and scholarly
writing, which is copyedited more anally than literature
or song lyrics. One reads in the *Chronicle of Higher Education,* "At some point, every academic who moves
into administration or association work has to set aside
their scholarship"; in an Associated Press news article of
"a law that prohibits commercial use of someone's name
or likeness without *their* consent"; in the *New York
Times,* "You have to know someone with a cellphone.
They can get the code for you"; and, in the academic
journal *American Speech,* "I urge every member of the
ADS [American Dialect Society] to unwrap *their* copies
of *Centennial Usage Studies.*" The *Shorter Oxford English
Dictionary,* published in 2002, includes as a definition of
they, "In relation to a singular noun or pronoun of un-
determined gender, *he or she.*" And on July 18, 2005,
the president of the United States said: "If someone

committed a crime, they will no longer work in my administration." You heard it here first: by the middle of the twenty-first century, the epicene *they* will rule in speech and writing.*

Anyway, the point should be clear. Pronouns matter. By definition, they are not strictly necessary; one can express any idea by using nouns or noun phrases. However, only three classes of people habitually eschew pronouns and if you do so, you will risk being regarded as belonging to one of them. The first is small children. The second is the parents of small children, who will say things like "Daddy wants Judy to eat her mashed bananas." (When my children were small, I actually refused to give up pronouns and insisted on saying "I" and "you." Perhaps this explains why my children, now

---

* But it will continue to be a two-steps-forward-one-step-back kind of thing. The fourteenth edition of *The Chicago Manual of Style*, published in 1993, stated that "the University of Chicago Press recommends the revival of the singular use of *they* and *their*." But the editors of the *Manual* removed this sentence in the 2003 fifteenth edition, replacing it with the noncommittal observation, "it is unacceptable to a great many readers . . . to use *they* as a singular pronoun." And yesterday at the doctor's office, I read on the cover of *Fit Pregnancy* magazine, "Protect Your Baby: Keep him safe from environmental dangers (even before he's born)." Interestingly, every single member of the magazine's editorial staff is female.

teenagers, appear to regard me as a figure of fun.)* The
third class is lawyers, whose prose puts a premium on
precision and who thus understandably want to avoid
any confusion concerning antecedents (the words pronouns take the place of). Such confusion is a real danger. In *The Pickwick Papers*, Sam Weller complains
about an "incomprehensible" letter: "Who's to know
wot it means, vith all this he-ing and I-ing!"

But attorneys sometimes take things too far. In his
book *Legal Language*, Peter M. Tiersma quotes a National Football League contract in which successive
sentences begin, "Player will report promptly for and
participate fully in Club's official pre-season training
camp. . . . If invited, Player will practice for and play in
any all-star football game. . . . Player will not participate in any football game not sponsored by the League."
Tiersma says of the repetition of *Player*: "There is only
one human male that this contract could possibly refer

---

* This brings up an interesting aspect of first- and second-person
pronouns. They don't just take the place of nouns but suggest a
whole dramatic situation. *I* or *we* implies a writer, a speaker, a
group the writer or speaker represents, or a group speaking in
unison; *you* implies a listener, a reader, or a group of listeners or
readers. Using nouns instead of these pronouns—saying to my
wife, for example, "Ben would like Gigi to walk the dog"—isn't
an option for adults.

to, so there is absolutely no danger in using *he* or *his* more often."

Many people would be less anxious about their own use of language if there were no pronouns, because this word class carries with it an awful lot of rules. Probably the biggest problem concerns case. Let's say I answer the phone and the voice on the other end says, "Is Ben Yagoda there?" If I have reason to think I'm being called by a direct marketer, I say, "No speak English," and hang up. But if it's a real person, how should I respond? Standard English mandates that the verb *be* be followed by the subjective case, which would have me say something like "This is he." Such a conjugation can have power, as in Matthew 14:22: "Straightway Jesus spake until them, saying, 'Be of good cheer; it is I; be not afraid.' " But in the current millennium, that kind of thing sounds fatally stuffy. This is obvious to songwriters, who have given us such works as Todd Rundgren's "Hello, It's Me" and (better yet) Crystal Gayle's "If Your Phone Doesn't Ring, It's Me"; to Shakespeare, who had Ophelia say, "Woe is me"; and to the writers of the King James Bible, who used the same statement three separate times, including Isaiah 6:5: "Then said I, Woe is me! for I am undone; because I am a man of unclean lips." Grammarian Randolph Quirk has observed that in uses other than immediately before the verb, the subjective case is "marked" (that is, seems to call attention to itself) and the objective case "unmarked" in English speech. In other words, "It is I" and "The teacher is he" and "We have met the enemy and he is we" all are technically correct but sound funny. To make them sound unmarked, or unremarkable, you have to embrace being "wrong" and replace the final word with *me*, *him*, or *us* —the last producing the famous quote from Walt Kelly's *Pogo*. (Getting back to the original phone-call question, I think "This is he" sounds pompous but "This is him" sounds louche; the common cop-out of "Speaking" makes me wonder why the individual feels he or she is too busy to talk in complete sentences. This was also the impression given in a documentary about O. J. "The Juice" Simpson I saw many years ago, in which he was shown picking up the phone and saying, "Juice. Go." Anyway, I usually cop out my own way and say something along the lines of "This is Ben.")

The gap between common and correct usage has had unfortunate consequences, including the practice known as "hypercorrection," which is a polite way of saying "wrong but with good intentions." People who have been yelled at so many times for saying things like "It's me" or "Me and Billy went to the store" hypercorrect by saying "My mother took Billy and I to the store" and "between you and I." The latter is undoubtedly a phrase that pushes people's buttons. It was the top vote getter in a 1986 BBC poll of listeners' pet language peeves, and James Cochrane used it as the title of his recent book about "bad English." Interestingly, however, such distinguished scholars as Noam Chomsky and Steven Pinker think it isn't so bad. Pinker defends Bill Clinton's 1992 plea that voters "give Al Gore and I a chance to bring America back," arguing that criticism of Clinton's use of *I* instead of *me* rests on a "false" assumption: that "if an entire conjunction phrase has a grammatical feature like subject case, every word inside that phrase has to have that feature, too." In other words "Al Gore and I" and "you and I" are *units* that can properly be used as the objective case, without changing the *I* to *me*. That's all well and good, but I don't see Pinker using "between you and I" in his own writing. He knows full well that if he did, he would sound like Miss Adelaide in *Guys and Dolls*.

Some people try to avoid the choice between subjective and objective by using a reflexive pronoun instead. As Red Smith noted: "*Myself* is the foxhole of ignorance where cowards take refuge because they were taught that *me* is vulgar and *I* is egotistical." I would also attribute part of *myself*'s popularity to the verbal self-indulgence that inspires people to say "utilize" instead of "use" and "at this point in time" instead of "now." In any case, it's fitting that Smith was a sportswriter, because the sports pages are where one finds quote after quote on the order of "I'm sure Ron and myself will have much better of stuff the rest of the season."

Some odd things have been happening to the first-person singular lately. For years, the possessive case has been used in juvenile contexts: "My Weekly Reader," "My Little Pony," "My First Bra" (an actual Web site), and so forth. Some time back, this construction got enthusiastically taken up in the dot-com world, so that a personal configuration of an online service is inevitably described in the form "My AOL," "My Yahoo," and "My Rhapsody." The trend in the first-person objective is its application to inanimate objects. Lewis Carroll may have started this in *Alice's Adventures in Wonderland*, where a cake is marked "Eat me" and a bottle "Drink me," but it was still worthy of remark in 1974, when I read a brief item in *Reader's Digest* that has always stuck with me. It described a truck with a sign reading, "Talk to me about better telephone service." Scrawled in the dust underneath were the words: "I don't talk to no truck."* Now such personification is commonplace, as you can see if you walk the aisles at Toys "R" Us and observe all the push-button toys whose packages command, "Try me." And of course, whenever you install or download a piece of software, you are directed to the "readme" file.

Now it's time for the number one most confusing pronoun question of all time. That's right, sports fans, I'm talking *who* or *whom*? By strange serendipity, in the middle of writing this paragraph, I was e-mailed an article from the *Chronicle of Higher Education* about the importance of connections in job hunting. The title is "Is It Whom You Know?" While this is "correct," it perfectly illustrates Calvin Trillin's remark, "As far as I'm concerned, 'whom' is a word that was invented to make everyone sound like a butler." As any grammar book will tell you, *whom* stands in for the objective case and *who* for the subjective. If you shift around the words in the sentence and can use *him* or *her*, then *whom* is called for, and if *he* or *she* is the choice, then you use *who*. Jon is the boy *whom* I hit; Jon is the boy *who* hit me. *Whom*

---

* I know all the details because I keyed "I don't talk to no truck" into Google and got the August 1974 edition of the *Newsletter of the Washington State Association of Data Processing Managers*, whose editor thought the item was amusing enough to reprint it.

is marked—and how. You can sometimes avoid that butler sound by merely leaving it out, as in "Jon is the boy I hit," an irreproachable sentence. But be warned: in certain cases the maneuver involves indulging in a sentence-ending preposition, as when "He's the person to whom I spoke" becomes "He's the person I spoke to." No such option is available when you ask a question that attempts to identify the object of some action. As far back as 1921, Edward Sapir observed that more and more, people were (incorrectly) choosing *who* to lead off such sentences; he predicted that not too far off in the future, "not even the most learned jurist will be saying, 'Whom did you see?' " We're not quite at that point yet, but we're close. Randolph Quirk and a colleague recorded 170,000 hours of "educated" people speaking English, and in all that talking, *whom* was used only nine times. However, no one used *who* incorrectly in its place, suggesting the popularity of the avoidance strategy.

The cleanup hitters of this part of speech are the personal pronouns in the subjective case. *It, I, you, he, they, she,* and *we* are respectively the eighth, eleventh, fourteenth, fifteenth, twenty-eighth, and thirty-third most frequently used words in the English language.

The popularity of *it* makes sense, because the word is not only a pronoun standing in for any nonhuman noun or noun phrase ("I bought this shirt yesterday, and I think it looks nice"), but also a potent dummy word in such common sentence types as "It looks like rain," "Tell it like it is," or "Take it easy." One hunts for the antecedent of such an *it* at one's own peril. In Carroll's *Alice's Adventures in Wonderland*, the Mouse begins to say that " 'the patriotic archbishop of Canterbury found it advisable—' "

> "Found *what?*" said the Duck.
>
> "Found *it*," the Mouse replied rather crossly: "of course you know what 'it' means."
>
> "I know what 'it' means well enough, when *I* find a thing," said the Duck: "it's generally a frog, or a worm. The question is, what did the archbishop find?"
>
> The Mouse did not notice this question, but hurriedly went on.

Nevertheless, the dummy *it* has a kind of existential resonance, which is why it's used in so many songs, titles, and ad slogans, including "You asked for it, we got it"; "I'm loving it"; and "It's the real thing." According to www.imdb.com, the comprehensive cinematic Web site, 166 film titles kick off with *It* or *It's*, including *It Came from Outer Space*, *It Happened One Night*, *It's a Wonderful Life*, *It's Alive*, and *It*—both the 1990 adaptation of Stephen King's novel about a scary clown and the 1927 silent film that gave Clara Bow the nickname "The It Girl." And indeed, *it* evokes both horror and sex, which deep down clearly have a lot in common. The Freudian concept of Id, referring to unbridled libido, is merely the Latin word for *it* and suggests this connection. So (possibly) does the fact that in the game of tag, the person run from is called It. Lately, the sexual connotation of the word has tended to predominate. In the 1920s, Cole Porter wrote "Birds do it, bees do it/Even educated fleas do it"; in the seventies, Bread recorded "I'd Like to Make It with You"; in the eighties, anonymous wags composed the bumper stickers "Teachers Do It with Class" and "Librarians Do It by the Book."

On the downside, *it* can lead writers into sticky wickets. Like *there*, the word lets you avoid finding precise active verbs and indulge in flabby constructions like "It is easy to see that it is better to do it differently." The Romantic-era writer William Cobbett advised, "Never put an *it* upon paper without thinking well of what you are about. When I see many *its* on a page, I always tremble for the writer."

Another problem is *its*, which has the distinction of being the only word in the language where a possessive is formed by adding *s* but not an apostrophe. It's (I'm using the contraction for *it is*, not the possessive) a relatively new word. Before about 1600, the most commonly used neuter possessives were *it* ("Sendeth the humour melencolyke to the stomacke for to prouoke it appetite"—Robert Copland, 1541) and *his* ("Aprille with hise shoures soote"—Chaucer), and for a couple of centuries after that, judging by the examples listed in the *OED*, apostrophes were an acceptable option (Shakespeare: "The Cradle-babe, Dying with mothers dugge betweene it's lips"). But then the unapostrophopic form became dominant, apparently to distinguish it from the contraction. Today, if you refer to "it's lips" you risk being mocked in a book like *Eats, Shoots & Leaves*.

The second-place finish of *I* would surprise no one who has noted the egocentrism of Western culture. Incidentally, etymologists agree that those of us who capitalize the word (basically, all of us, except E. E. Cummings and the legion of high school poets in his thrall, Don Marquis, and a disquieting number of my e-mail correspondents) do so for reasons of typography rather than ego. The Old English *ic* or *ich* had developed into a one-letter pronoun by the middle of the twelfth century, and within about a hundred years it came to be written with a capital letter so as to avoid the misreading of handwritten manuscripts.

The capitalization of *I* may be why it makes many people so uncomfortable. Yet an expression or acknowledgment of self is often welcome in prose. Consider the opening lines of two classic American novels: "Call me Ishmael" and "You don't know about me without you have read a book by the name of *The Adventures of Tom Sawyer*; but that ain't no matter." "I am an American, Chicago-born," which kicks off Saul Bellow's *The Adventures of Augie March*, isn't half bad, either. And Whitman's *Leaves of Grass*? "One's-self I sing—a simple, separate Person." It's not just a literary thing, the banishment or extreme disapproval of *I* that you find in scientific, legal, and journalistic writing (where it's disparaged as "the vertical pronoun") is a case of hypercorrection. It leads to overuse of the passive voice, in all its opaque unaccountability; to silly formulations like "the present researcher" and "this reporter"; and to book critics saying things like "the reader is disappointed" when they would do better to proclaim and stand behind their own reactions.

In contrast to this fraudulent humility, *I* is sometimes avoided because just the one letter isn't grand enough. Old-fashioned phrases like "yours truly" and "your humble and obedient servant" are examples, as is a current formulation I call the third-person athletic—the odd liking ballplayers have of referring to themselves by their names or nicknames. The current champion performer is footballer Terrell Owens, clearly a linguistic pioneer, who raised the bar to a new height when he said, "Eight-One is going to be on the field," eighty-one being his uniform number.

More commonly, people pluralize themselves. Thoreau said that *we* should be used only by royalty, editors, pregnant women, and people who ate worms, but additional categories have been added since his time. *The New Yorker*'s "Talk of the Town" section was famously written in the anonymous first-person plural for more than six decades, its items leading off with improbable sentences like "With the city water supply teetering, as of Saturday, at the hundred-per-cent mark, we went down to the Municipal Building to see if officials of the Department of Water Supply, Gas, and Electricity were pleased with the situation." (When Tina Brown became editor of the magazine in 1993, she introduced both the first-person singular and bylines into "Talk of the Town," causing much wailing and gnashing of teeth.) There are also the much-maligned medical we ("How are we feeling today?"), the "workshop we" (a term coined by grammarian Katie Wales, in her book *Personal Pronouns in*

Present-Day English, for pompous exposition like "if we are to talk about metaphor we shall at some point need a term . . ."), and the "Elvis we," a termed coined by yours truly. It occurs when people unencumbered by modesty—usually athletes, entertainers, or politicians—follow the King's lead and say things like "All we ask is to be on time, play hard and play together" (basketball coach P. J. Carlesimo), "We decided it was time for us to expand" (Jesse Jackson), and "We are a grandmother," a notoriously royalesque statement made by former British prime minister Margaret Thatcher. The perfect reply to every one of the above statements, I would say, is a rhetorical question favored by a college buddy of mine: "You got a rat in your pocket?" Somewhat more acceptable in polite company is the punch line to the classic joke about the Lone Ranger and Tonto being surrounded by hostile Indians. Lone Ranger: "What are we going to do, Tonto?" Tonto: "What you mean *we*, kemo sabe?"

Yet another ploy for meaning *I* without saying it is the word *one*. This, however, is the exclusive province of the British royalty and upper class, and sounds faintly ridiculous when used by anyone else. Come to think of it, it even sounds faintly ridiculous when used by the British royalty and upper class. Listen to Prince Charles: "It was a sad moment leaving one's family on

the tarmac, waving one goodbye." Waving one good-
bye? Margaret Thatcher loved to indulge in this sort of
thing, as when she said to a reporter, "Already one finds
oneself taking the most forceful leadership role because
of . . . one's own style."

To which one can only quote Fats Waller: "One
never knows, do one?"

One is more commonly used as Waller and I just did—
to mean something like "a person" or, informally, *you*. The
word can be useful, as long as one is okay with coming off
a bit hoity-toity. *One* is also a thorny antecedent. That is,
unless you want to repeat the word, as Waller did, you're
faced with saying "One never knows, does he?" (sexist);
"One never knows, does he or she?" (does not sound like
English); or "One never knows, do they?" (nuh-uh).

The fact that *you* follows closely behind *I* in popularity is probably attributable to its being an eight-way
word: both subject and object, both singular and plural,
and both formal and familiar. The all-purpose second
person is an unusual feature of English, as middle-
schoolers realize when they start taking French, Spanish, or, especially, German, which offers a choice of
seven different singular versions of *you*. It's relatively
new in our language. In early modern English, beginning in the late fifteenth century, *thou*, *thee*, and *thy*
were singular forms for the subjective, objective, and

possessive, and *ye*, *you*, and *your* were plural.* In the 1500s and 1600s, *ye*, and then the *thou/thee/thy* forms, faded away, to be replaced by the all-purpose *you*. But approaches to the second person were interesting in this period of flux. David Crystal writes in *The Cambridge Encyclopedia of English* that by Shakespeare's time, *you* "was used by people of lower rank or status to those above them (such as ordinary people to nobles, children to parents, servants to masters, nobles to the monarch), and was also the standard way for the upper classes to talk to each other. By contrast, *thou/thee* were used by people of higher rank to those beneath them, and by the lower classes to each other; also, in elevated poetic style, in addressing God, and in talking to witches, ghosts, and other supernatural beings." The *OED* cites a 1675 quotation: "No Man will *You* God, but will use the pronoun *Thou* to him."

Needless to say, this ambiguity and variability were gold in the hand of a writer like Shakespeare, and he played with it endlessly, sometimes having a character

---

* The *ye* that's used in self-consciously quaint names like "Ye Olde Antique Shoppe" is completely different. When printing presses came to England, blocks generally were not made for a letter, called *thon*, that had been used for *th* sounds. It was usually replaced by putting the letters *t* and *h* together, but sometimes *y* was used because it was felt to look similar.

switch modes of address within a speech to indicate a change in attitude. Crystal cites Sir Toby Belch's advice to Sir Andrew Aguecheek, in *Twelfth Night*, on how to get under the skin of an antagonist: "if thou thou'st him some thrice, it will not be amiss." Sir Toby, of course, is himself thou-ing Sir Andrew.

Other than in wedding ceremonies, translations from languages with second-person familiar (for example, Martin Buber's *I and Thou*), and ironic juxtaposition (Rodgers and Hart's "Thou Swell"), the old form persists only in the language of the Society of Friends, a.k.a. the Quakers, who revived it in the seventeenth century because they considered *you* to be an expression of vanity and corruption. The rest of the world often found this attitude annoying. George Fox wrote in his journal that he and fellow Friends were "in danger many times of our lives, and often beaten, for using those words to some proud men, who would say, 'Thou'st "thou" me, thou ill-bred clown.' "

The only problem presented by the all-purpose second person is in the plural. It's useful to be able to differentiate between addressing a person and a group, which is why so many unofficial plural forms have sprung up. Katie Wales lists *yin* (Scottish), *youse* (she locates it in Northern England and Dublin, but I would add Philadelphia), *guys* or *you guys* (U.S., and non-specific as to gender), *yousuns* (Hiberno-English), *you together* (East Anglian), and *you all* (Southern American). There are many others, including *yiz*, *everybody*, *you people*, and the middle-class British *you lot*, which Wales, a professor at the University of London, may have felt too unremarkable to include.

You all—sometimes spelled, and pronounced, *y'all*—which white Southerners adopted from African Americans as late as the mid-nineteenth century, is the most famous form, and also the most controversial. A 1989 bibliography listed twenty-five scholarly articles on the term, of which seventeen, amazingly, addressed a single issue: whether anyone ever addresses a single person with the term. The view that it is used that way only by Yankee screenwriters and never by real Southerners, H. L. Mencken observed in *The American Language*, "is a cardinal article of faith in the South, and questioning it is almost as serious a *faux pas* as hinting that General Lee was an octoroon." Sadly, most of those articles offer no hard evidence—one camp shouting, in so many words, "I've heard it used as a singular!"; the other, "I've never heard it used as a singular!" An exception is a recent study reporting the results of a survey of more than five hundred Oklahomans, of whom about 30 percent confirmed that yes, they had indeed used *y'all* or *you all* to refer to just one person.*

Moving on to the third-person singular, the fact that *he* is used almost twice as often as *she* (6,810 versus 3,801 times per million words in one corpus) provides useful ammunition for anyone arguing that we still live in a sexist society. Beyond that, the two words are fairly straightforward, though not quite as much so as they might appear. They provide, for one thing, a sneaky way to express disapproval or disrespect. A traditionally appealing rhetorical strategy for adolescents in reference to their parents, this leads to the classic dinnertable rebuke "Don't refer to your mother as she!" or, in England, "Who's 'she,' the cat's grandmother?"† On the notorious "Squidgy" tape of Princess Diana conversing with her lover, she always refers to Prince Charles as "he," as if saying his name would be more than she could bear. James Atlas, the biographer of Saul Bellow, had a hard time coming up with a pronoun when his

* Jan Tillery and Guy Bailey, "Yall in Oklahoma," *American Speech*, 73, no. 3, Autumn 1998.
† But how *can* a kid, in conversation with one parent, refer to the other parent and still retain some dignity? That is, saying "Mother," "Mom," or "Mommy" doesn't really make sense, as she *isn't* the mom of the person being addressed. Saying "my mother" sounds odd too. I leave this question to Miss Manners.

subject was not present and he was speaking with Mrs. Bellow. "He" sounded disrespectful, "Saul" too familiar, and "Mr. Bellow" too subservient. The slightly ironic and vaguely Irish-sounding "himself" has sometimes been used in such situations, but I admire Atlas's solution: "the great man."

The third-person plural is the favorite pronoun of racists, paranoids, and adherents to the conventional wisdom; people spend whole lifetimes thinking in terms of what this unnamed and undefined group says and does. A current bestseller, which has the decency to put the word in quotation marks, is *Natural Cures "They" Don't Want You to Know About*. Bruce Springsteen skillfully uses the word to portray the sense his narrators have of a world controlled by outside, mostly malevolent, forces. His song "Johnny 99" opens, "Well they closed down the auto plant in Mahwah late that month," and in "Atlantic City" he tells us that "they blew up the chicken man in Philly last night,/Now they blew up his house too/Down on the boardwalk they're gettin' ready for a fight,/Gonna see what them racket boys can do."

"Them racket boys." The phrase leads me to my last pronoun exploration, of the word *that* and its cousins. The seventh most frequently used word in the language, *that* has four kinds of meanings. The first is as a

conjunction ("I told him that the book is very good"),
already treated, and the second as an adverb, as in "I
didn't think it was going to be that hot today." The final two are pronouns. Along with *this*, *these*, and *those*,
that is a demonstrative used either by itself ("What's
that you're doing?") or right before a noun ("I'm interested in that car over there.")* The difference between
this and *that*, obviously, is one of physical or conceptual
distance; what's not always so clear is where one's territory stops and the other's begins. (Something you're
holding is a *this*, something out of sight is a *that*, but a
visible object not on one's person could be either one.)
There used to be a third demonstrative: *yon*, from the
same root as *yonder*, and indicating something far away.
Yon fell out of use in the eighteenth century, and people who affect it today are being self-consciously archaic, like the legendary Philadelphia disk jockey Jerry
Blavat, who addresses his listeners as "yon teens." Even
including *yon*, English demonstratives are comparatively simple. In *The Story of Language*, Mario Pei points
out that "Ilocano, a tongue of the Philippines, has three
words for *this* referring to a visible object, a fourth for

---

* Some dictionaries and grammar books categorize this *that* as a
determiner, and others as an adjective.

things not in view and a fifth for things that no longer exist."

Getting back to Springsteen's line, the demonstrative is, for some reason, very susceptible to colloquial uses, where it packs a wallop. A 1989 survey of British speakers identified the replacement of demonstrative *those* with *them* as the single most common feature of nonstandard English. It was still in the lexicon ten years later when English national soccer coach Glen Hoddle, alleged to have made insensitive comments about disabled people, told an interviewer: "But at this moment in time I did not say them things and at the end of the day I want to put that on record because it has hurt people." The usage is just as common in the United States vernacular; the *New York Times* recently permitted pitcher Andy Pettite to say in its pages, "They probably took a picture with just them four." Even more popular here than across the pond is *them* as an unaccompanied demonstrative ("Them that's got shall get/Them that's not shall lose"—Billie Holiday's "God Bless the Child") and the variants *this here*, *that there*, and *them there* (the location of the hills where gold is supposed to be).

The fourth and final use of *that* is as a relative pronoun: "*The Best and the Brightest* is the book that got me interested in politics." One tricky thing for many people is the question of whether to use *that* or *which* in such a sentence, in which the pronoun precedes what is called a defining or restrictive clause. I hesitate to add to the thousands of pages that (or is it which?) have been written on the subject, so will merely and briefly try to be helpful to the perplexed. Both *that* and *which* are grammatically acceptable and historically widespread. Great and not-so-great writers have used both, including in the same sentence, as in the King James Bible: "Render therefore unto Caesar the things which are Caesar's; and unto God the things that are God's." However, in the nineteenth century, official sentiment—crystallized in Fowler's *Modern English Usage*—began to favor *that*, and this preference is still reflected in most grammar and style guides. So be warned: you may run into *which*-hunting professors, editors, or bosses.

I confess a prejudice against *that* when the defining or restrictive clause refers to a human being, as in a quotation from Lance Armstrong: "I'm a kid from Texas that learned how to ride a bike fast." Books like *Merriam-Webster's Dictionary of English Usage* tell me there's a long history of writers putting *that* instead of *who* in the blank—even good writers; Twain called his novella *The Man That Corrupted Hadleyburg*—but I don't have to like it. On the evidence of its increasing frequency in my students' work, I believe that, like the epicene *they*, it's a colloquialism that has crept into writing and will one day dominate.

Getting back to the *that–which* question, *which* is the unequivocal choice when the clause following it is non-defining or nonrestrictive or (as the *Associated Press Stylebook* helpfully puts it) nonessential. The presence of a comma is also a clue that *which* is called for. So you would write "I went to Horace Mann School, which is the alma mater of a lot of interesting people," or "We are done with relative pronouns, which is a good thing."

But while we're on the subject of *which*, here's one more question. To lead off an interrogative sentence, when do you use *what* and when do you use *which*? I confess (I seem to be in a confessing mood) that this had always perplexed me, and so I'm pleased to have found out, and to report the answer. *What* is preferred when the choice is open or indefinite, as when someone looks around the library and asks, "What book should I read?" *Which* is called for when the number of alternatives is small. Looking over the dessert tray, one rhetorically asks, "Which should I pick?"

That's all, you guys.

CHAPTER IX

V. Adj. Adv. Art. Conj. Int. N. Prep. Pron.

MAN STEPPING INTO A TAXI AT BOSTON'S LOGAN AIRPORT: Do you know where I can get scrod around here?

CABDRIVER: I've been driving a hack for thirty years, and that's the first time I've ever heard it in the pluperfect subjunctive.

—*Popular joke*

The fact is I think I am a verb instead of a personal pronoun. A verb is anything that signifies to be; to do; or to suffer. I signify all three.

—*Ulysses S. Grant*

Last alphabetically, the verb is in every other way the foremost part of speech—starting with the fact that its etymological root is *verbum*, the Latin word for word. Without verbs we would be grunting out nouns and making crude hand gestures to explain what we think about or want done with them. Verbs are the basis of grammar, and their accidence and conjugation let us express our complicated and peculiarly human ideas about each other and the world. As Michael Maittaire wrote in 1712, "It is the only Word, which gives motion and life to all the rest; without which there can be no sentences, and all other words are but like a rope of sand, without any sense at all."

On one level, the English verb system is simple. In Latin, a verb has up to 120 inflections, or forms. English regular verbs have only four: for the verb *to cook*, they would be *cook, cooks, cooked, cooking*. Some verbs have a mere trio, for example, *to cut: cut, cuts, cutting*. And none has more than the five of *to see: see, sees, saw, seeing*, and *seen*. English expresses inflection or mood through a series of remarkable little words known as auxiliary, or helping, verbs: *be, can, could, do, have, may, might, must, shall, should, will*, and *would*. When put in front of a main verb, these words can indicate a dizzying array of meanings, including future occurrence (*will, shall*), ability (*can, could*), conditionality (*would*), possibility (*may, might*), and lots of others. A verb can be preceded by one auxiliary ("I *may* take a nap this afternoon"), two ("She *has been* taking yoga for twelve years"), three ("That *could have been* our only chance"), or even four ("He *must have been being* tackled when he spat out his mouthguard").

Worthy of special mention are *be, have*, and *do*. First

of all, unlike the other auxiliaries, they can do double duty as main verbs. *Be* helps form the progressive tenses ("I am/was going") and the passive voice ("The song was sung"), and *have* the perfect tenses ("I have/had gone"). You can see some of the many functions of the verb *to do* in the following exchange: "What *did* you say?" "You *didn't* wash your hands." "Yes, I *did*." "*Don't* contradict me." The word is needed for asking questions and making negative statements or commands; in the third sentence, it serves as a kind of verb pronoun, standing in for *wash*.*

The auxiliaries have a bunch of strange and singular attributes. Unlike main verbs, they can be used before the word *not* ("You should not go") without sounding archaic, and, in a question, before the subject of a sentence ("Have they left yet?"). In fact, they are pretty much necessary for the formations of questions; otherwise, you come out with queries like "Eat you lunch with me today?" Also (except for *be*, *have*, and *do*), they have only one form. In other words, *must* appears as nothing other than *must*; there are no such words as *musts*, *musted*, *to must*, or *musting*. Sometimes people try

---

* The British take this further than we Yanks, appending a *do* or *have done* to auxiliary verbs. "Nigel didn't thank Reg for the tea cozy." "Well, he should have done."

to correct this limitation. American Southerners, for example, try to create a sort of future tense of *might* by saying things like "I might could come by tomorrow." Bryan Garner claims this is the same thing as "I might come by tomorrow," but it really isn't. Other such "double modals" are *might can*, *might should*, and *might would*. There are similar expressions for the past tense, such as *used to could*, *used to didn't*, and *used to was*. These expressions are so colorful, pungent, and useful that I might would adopt them, except that I've spent my whole life within 105 miles of New York City.

The second most commonly used nonauxiliary verb (*see* is first), and by far the most common in conversation, is *get*. I love this word, not least for its dizzying array of meanings. Anthony Burgess once listed some of the many uses to which it can be put: "I get up in the morning, get a bath and a shave, get dressed, get my breakfast, get into the car, get to the office, get down to work, get some coffee at eleven, get lunch at one, get back, get angry, get tired, get home, get into a fight with my wife, get to bed." A lot of these, admittedly, are specific variations on *obtain* ("get my breakfast"), *arrive* ("get home"), or *become* ("get angry," "the play got boring"). But the word has many other denotations, and my daughter Maria and I sometimes amuse ourselves trying to add to our running list (we're easily amused).

Get can be an alternative for *receive* ("I get a lot of junk mail"), *retrieve* (in the imperative mood—"Get the ball"), *start* ("Get going"), *persuade* ("I got my father to stop talking about *get*"), *nab* ("The cops got the criminal," "He got the girl"), *understand* ("He just doesn't get it"), *annoy* ("The way she keeps clearing her throat really gets me"), *succeed* ("I finally got the faucet to stop leaking"), and a kind of combination of *to be allowed* and *to manage*: "I got to shake the pope's hand." And get a load of this: in a restaurant you might say, "Can I get a cup of coffee?" or "You paid yesterday—today I'll get the check." *Get* can also be a sort of general verb of agency ("She got him drunk") and can serve as a substitute for the passive-voice *to be*: "I got hit upside the head." Other meanings are found in the song "Get Down Tonight" (part of a panoply of sexual *gets*, including *get lucky*, *get laid*, and *get off*), the idioms "get rid of" and "get over it," expressions in the form of "get your laugh on," and the eloquent one-word command "Get!"—otherwise known as "Git!"

Some people tsk-tsk whenever they hear *get*, but the foregoing usage is all perfectly okay. Things can get grammatically problematic, however, when the word is used either together with or as a substitute for the verb *have*. For one thing, its past participle is the only one I know that differs according to what side of the Atlantic you're on. Reviewing a book that compares 1962 and 2004, the Englishman Nicholas Lezard says, "You find yourself asking what has got better in the intervening time." Americans would say "*gotten* better"—except Americans writing in *The New Yorker* (long accused of Anglophilia), where we find Louis Menand observing, "We have all got a little smarter since then, but the people who work in movie publicity have got a lot smarter," and Joan Acocella wondering how a mismatched couple in a Zadie Smith novel could have "got together."

We do say *have got*, in, for example, AOL's "You've got mail," Oscar Hammerstein's lyric "You've got to be taught to hate," Bob Dylan's lyric "You've got a lot of nerve to say you are my friend," and the sports compliment "You've got game." If you examine all those sentences, you will see that as long as you stretch out *you've* to *you have*, the *got* is superfluous. But you will also see that they would be immeasurably weaker with *have* as the sole verb. At one time *have got* was looked down on as an "inelegant expression" (in the words of John Bechtel's 1896 book *Slips of Speech*), but it's now accepted. Even Henry Higgins in *My Fair Lady* says, "I think she's [that is, she has] got it." Americans, however, have taken things one step further and like to eliminate the *have*. When done with other

participles—"I been coming here for twenty years"—
such a maneuver is dicey. And, on the printed page, a
naked *got* appears a bit déclassé; in *The Great Gatsby*,
Fitzgerald shows Myrtle Wilson's coarseness by having
her say, "I got to call up my sister." But in speech it's
okay, and it adds bite to song titles including "Got to
Get You into My Life," "I Got It Bad (And That Ain't
Good)," "Got to Be There," "I Got Plenty of Nuthin',"
and "I Got Rhythm" (the last two by that master of the
vernacular Ira Gershwin), to Tug McGraw's stirring
quote "You gotta believe," and to the universal baseball
cry "I got it!" (Allegedly the longtime coach at the
fancy New York day school Horace Mann, my alma
mater, insisted that his players instead say, "I have it!,"
which must have produced quite a few smirks from the
opposing nine from Poly Prep.)

Got = *have* took a giant leap forward in 1993, when
a San Francisco ad agency came up with the dairy slogan "Got milk?" This struck a nerve, and then some.
Writing recently in the *Fort Worth Star-Telegram*,
Robert Philpot listed some borrowings of the motto:

A billboard for Tide laundry detergent asks, "Got
napkins?" A newspaper ad for Luby's Cafeteria recently inquired, "Got fish?" A billboard for Fort
Worth-Dallas sports-talk radio station KTCK-AM

(1310) asks, "Got sports?" And a doormat asks the question, "Got wine?" Some ads even ask us if we've got stuff we "don't" want, such as a weight-loss formula ad that poses the question, "Got fat?" And then there are the non sequitur questions, such as the one posed by a recent "TV Guide" cover about the sitcom "Malcolm in the Middle," which asked, "Got Malcolm?"

Philpot reported that the California Milk Processor Board, which commissioned the campaign, keeps an ever-lengthening in-house list titled "Got Ripped Off?"

To get is a member in good standing of the English language's body of about two hundred irregular verbs. For the most part, what makes a verb irregular is that its past form and/or its participial form are *not* formed the way they are in regular verbs: merely by adding *-ed* to the main verb. So you have conjugations like *get/got/gotten, be/was/been, have/had/had, do/did/done, say/said/said, make/made/made, go/went/gone, see/saw/seen, know/knew/known,* and *take/took/taken.* I have just listed the ten most commonly used nonauxiliary verbs in the language, and in fact irregular verbs tend to be very popular and very old. (The most recent irregular to enter English language is *snuck*, which is an acceptable variation of *sneaked* as the past tense of *to* *sneak,* and which the *OED* notes as first appearing in 1887.) In his fascinating book on the subject, *Words and Rules,* Steven Pinker notes that 70 percent of the time we use a verb, we choose an irregular one, and that virtually all irregular verbs are one syllable in length.* However, irregular verbs make up a tiny minority of the word class. The regulars are especially overwhelming when it comes to the least common verbs, accounting for 98 percent of the verbs used only once in a million-word database. Without a doubt, irregular verbs are cool and add an element of unpredictability and liveliness to the language. It's no coincidence that in Orwell's *1984,* the state has banned them.

No one has any problem conjugating regular verbs, even when they don't actually mean anything. That is, if you give people a sentence like "Paul was plarking the dog" and ask what Paul did to the dog, 100 percent would say, "He plarked it." However, nonstandard or vernacular language systems, notably African American Vernacular English (AAVE), tend to make the regular verbs even *more* regular by eliminating the special conjugation for the third-person singular in the

---

* The exceptions are *understand, forget,* and *become,* which take their conjugations from the one-syllable irregulars *stand, get,* and *come.*

present tense. This is, or can be, pungent and striking. The first line of Jerry Butler's 1960 hit song ("He don't love you like I love you") and the enigmatic and haunting words football player Rod Smart once wrote on the back of his jersey, "He Hate Me," would be blander than bland if they were, instead, "He doesn't love you . . ." and "He Hates Me." I don't think I have ever read a lovelier poem than the note that was sent back with my older daughter at the end of her first week at day care: "Elizabeth had a nice day. Elizabeth always have a nice day."

Irregular verbs, by contrast, are difficult. If you look at the ten most popular ones listed above, you'll see that none of them even follows the same pattern for conjugation. Little kids and others trying to learn English will often regularize the past tense of irregulars, saying someone "hided" the ball or "hitted" another kid or (echoing the catchphrase of comedian Red Skelton's character The Mean Widdle Kid) "I dood it." Then there's Ralph on *The Simpsons*, who shared, "Once, I picked my nose till it bleeded." Mistakes made by adult native speakers usually consist of conjugating one irregular verb according to the pattern of *another* irregular verb. Neil Diamond famously referred to the "song she sang to me, song she brang to me." In the 2003 HBO documentary *Born Rich* a young socialite (speaking of

an exclusive club she belongs to) applies the *-en* participle suffix you find in *given* and *taken* to a verb that
doesn't call for it: "I brought three or four Jewish friends
to the Bathing Corp. today for lunch. And it's fine, I
mean, actually I don't know, that's the first time I've
ever broughten anyone, so who knows?"

Sometimes the "mistake" is completely intentional—
the variant is used not because people can't get the correct participle through their head but because the new
word supplies emphasis or nuance. Thus you hear
broughten fairly often in youth and street talk. One contributor to www.urbandictionary.com provides a translation of an exchange from the film *Not Another Teen
Movie*: "Bring it on, bitch." (*Because I do not like you, I invite you to fight me.*) "Oh, it has already been broughten."
(*I had already planned on fighting you.*) The Rick Moranis
movie is called *Honey I Shrunk the Kids* because someone,
somewhere along the way, divined that this sounded
somehow stronger and funnier than (the correct) *Honey
I Shrank the Kids*.

On the other hand, prosecutor Christopher Darden,
interrogating a witness in the O. J. Simpson trial, asked,
"So the gloves appeared to have shrank somewhat?"
One suspects this sprang (not sprung) from another
long tradition in AAVE, eschewing the standard participle. Usually that manifests itself, as in the Darden

example, with a simple substitution of the past tense: "We would have came." "He had went," etc. But there are other variations. In Lorraine Hansberry's *A Raisin in the Sun*, the character Walter says: "Mama, you know it's all divided up. Life is. Sure enough. Between the takers and the 'tooken.' "

AAVE is hardly alone in this; it's a characteristic of most nonstandard forms of English. Dizzy Dean, who was born in 1910 in Arkansas and grew up there and in Oklahoma, was a baseball star and later an announcer famous for such conjugations as *to swing: swing, swanged, swung.* He once defended himself by asserting, "And as for saying 'Rizzuto slid into second' it just ain't natural. Sounds silly to me. Slud is something more than slid. It means sliding with great effort." Nor did Dean back down. After retiring, he gave a speech titled "Radio Announcing I Have Did."

If Dizzy Dean didn't exist, Ring Lardner would have invented him. Or would *of* invented him, as Lardner would of put it. A typical sentence in his 1916 novel *You Know Me Al*, which consists of letters from bush-league baseball player Jack Keefe to a friend back home: "I wish he could of got the girl I married instead of the one he got and I bet she would of drove him crazy." In this same chapter Jack says, "if you had of went"; "if it had of been"; and "if I had of had." It takes a while for the extent of Jack's deviation from standard English to sink in. The respectable versions of those phrases are "if you had gone"; "if it had been"; and "if I had had." In other words, in addition to mixing up past and participial forms and substituting *of* for *have*, Lardner has Jack stick in an unnecessary *of/have*.

I make a point of this because in the years since 1916, that usage has become not necessarily standard but very, very common in speech. In her definitive *American Speech* article "If He Would Have and If He Didn't," Cecily Raysor Hancock cites, among many other examples, two newspaper quotations (the second, you will note, using the epicene pronoun): "If that elevator *would have* fallen down, that car would have been destroyed" and "A few years ago if someone *would have* told me that I would have four pigs living in my home I would have said they were crazy." Standard English would replace the italicized words with *had*, because a reference to a past condition contrary to fact, a subset of the subjunctive mood, takes the past perfect, or pluperfect, tense. The nonstandard usage probably arose because the normal subjunctive is unmarked and bland; the extra *would* is a pleonasm, that is, a rhetorical redundancy (and echoes the form of present-moment wishes, as in, "If only he would notice me"). It's a bit trickier in cases where the hypothetical event being discussed is negative. Reviewing an electronic device on a Web shopping site, someone wrote, "If I didn't get it for free, I'd feel cheated." The standard American English "If I hadn't gotten it for free" is stilted, but "If I wouldn't have gotten it for free" doesn't sound right. Sometimes people say, "If I hadn't have gotten it for free" (a pleonasm that has been dubbed the plupluperfect tense), but the more common maneuver is to do as this writer did and go straight to the past tense.

In recent years this usage has expanded from discussions of hypothetical past conditions (starting with *if*) to expressions of regret about the past. Let's say you're an English singer-songwriter who wants to express how sad you are that you never got a chance to be Marilyn Monroe's pal. In addressing the late actress in song, you have three options: 1) "I would have liked to have known you"; 2) "I would have liked to know you"; and 3) "I would like to have known you." Number 1 dominates the vernacular and was in fact was used by Elton John's lyricist Bernie Taupin in "Candle in the Wind." Football coach Andy Reid used it when he said, "I would have liked to have gotten Reggie a catch, but it didn't work out that way." Number 2 is the "correct" version, advocated by Garner and other authorities, and is okay, though I think the gerund is better than the infinitive— that is, "I would have liked knowing you." The problem is that nobody ever uses number 3, and it expresses a useful and distinct meaning. The first two examples refer to what the speaker would have felt *in the past* had the hypothetical taken place: something like "I would have enjoyed knowing you." Number 3, by contrast, describes a present state of mind, akin to wishing, and it's a useful thing to be able to describe, darn it. Most people say, "I would have liked to have attended his funeral" when they wouldn't have liked it at all. What they mean is "I would like to have attended the funeral."

There's still another verb option for past hypotheticals—the present tense. This is often chosen in a rhetorical arena that is uniquely given to discussions about what would have, could have, or should have happened. The arena is sports, and there's even a name for this kind of discourse: Monday Morning Quarterbacking. Sportswriters, desperate for copy, obsessively ask athletes to speculate. They respond by saying things like (these are all actual quotes): "It's a different game if we score"; "If they score on that one, they lose 49–10"; and "That ball is a single at Fenway. It hits the wall and bounces off." (This last was said by Dwight Evans of the Boston Red Sox, analyzing a home run he hit in the 1986 World Series against the New York Mets.)

These jocks, aside from expressing their thoughts with admirable conciseness, are also participating in a broad literary trend. The last few decades of the twentieth century saw a resurgence of the present tense that is still under way. For a very long time, this verb form was used for specific and limited purposes, including to indicate a current or habitual action ("I see you," "The sun rises in the east"); to tell an anecdote ("So I say to him . . .") or a joke ("A man walks into a bar"); to write newspaper headlines ("Man Bites Dog"); or to describe action or stage directions in a play script or screenplay. There was also the "historical present," employed to describe long-dead writers ("Milton compares good and evil in many different ways"), by portentous lecturers and *March of Time* narrators ("Napoleon arrives in Arles only to find . . ."), and very occasionally in historical writing and in fiction—for example in Dickens's *Bleak House*, where it added to the foggy mood of the narration. When Joyce Cary used the device in the 1939 novel *Mr. Johnson*, he felt compelled to justify it in a preface: "As Johnson swims gaily on the surface of life, so I wanted the reader to swim."

The tense flexed its muscles a couple of decades later. John Updike's original full title for his groundbreaking 1960 work was *Rabbit, Run: A Screenplay*, and even when he changed it to a novel he kept the present tense, not only for cinematic feel but because it suited the protagonist, Harry Angstrom, to whom things happen so fast that he's left bewildered. Binx Bolling and Bob Slocum, the alienated narrators of Walker Percy's and Joseph Heller's novels *The Moviegoer* and *Something Happened*, both published not long after *Rabbit, Run*, speak in the present tense for similar reasons—to describe what has happened to them in the past tense would somehow imply they've understood or accepted it.

For a couple of centuries journalists used the past tense exclusively: what power and authority they had depended on being able to attest to what they saw and what happened. Then Tom Wolfe came along. In the early sixties, Wolfe started building his feature newspaper and magazine stories out of a series of present-tense scenes. From a 1964 Wolfe profile of socialite Baby Jane Holzer: "Inez, the maid, brings in lunch on a tray, one rare hamburger, one cheeseburger and a glass of tomato juice. Jane tastes the tomato juice. 'Oh—!' she says. 'It's diet.' " Before long Wolfe's innovation began to trickle down to other journalists, who used it at first to copy him, then as a reflex action. Today, the default format for any slick magazine article is a series of scenes in the present tense.

Then the present invaded the short story. A key figure is Ann Beattie, whose 1974 story "Vermont" begins:

> Noel is in our living room shaking his head. He refuses my offer and then David's offer of a drink, but

> he has had three glasses of wine. It is absurd to won-
> der at such a time when he will get up to go to the
> bathroom, but I do.

The sound of these sentences, and others published by Beattie in *The New Yorker* and the collections *Distortions* and *Secrets and Surprises*, was unbelievably influential. As with Wolfe and the journalists, other writers got the memo, and soon the present was the default tense in short fiction. What was the appeal? I once had the opportunity to ask Ms. Beattie about the tense and she said she used it in her early stories for no reason other than that she imagined her scenes so vividly; she merely put down on paper what she was "literally seeing in front of my eyes." And, indeed, the present gives a strong feeling of immediacy; it mimics the feel of the movies, maybe the preeminent narrative form of the twentieth century. On a more subtle level, the present conveys some of the indeterminacy and randomness people seem to feel nowadays.

Poetry had picked up on this a bit earlier; indeed, the present is the characteristic tense of modern verse. Matthew Arnold's 1867 "Dover Beach," which has been called the first modern poem, begins: "The sea is calm to-night./The tide is full . . ." T. S. Eliot wrote in 1917, "In the room the women come and go/Talking of

Michelangelo." You can hear in that line the same attitude Paul McCartney was channeling when he wrote,
"Your day breaks/Your mind aches/You find that all her
words of kindness linger on when/She no longer needs
you." The tendency has only accelerated with time. Editor Peter Davison said in a recent *New York Times* interview, "Something like 70 percent of all the poems I
receive seem to be written in the present indicative.
They are constantly producing a sort of spectator poetry
in which the poet is looking at himself: 'I go out, I look
at the wires, there's snow on the wires, a blue jay sits on
the wires and knocks off some snow, God I'm lonely.' "

The present tense is undeniably effective, but, as
Davison's comment suggests, it's limiting. When you
can say, in the words of the (nineteenth-century) poet
Walt Whitman, "I am the man, I suffer'd, I was there,"
you assume authority. The past tense brings with it a
faith in the possibility of interpreting an orderly world,
beliefs that are apparently ever harder to sustain. By
contrast, the present tense gives us something along the
lines of a big database of human experience. Take it or
leave it.

In contrast to the present tense, some verb forms appear to be falling by the wayside. One is use of the subjunctive form of the verb *to be* to describe conditions

contrary to fact. Nowadays, people are likely to say, and maybe even write, "If my big brother was here, he would beat you up" instead of the standard and traditional "If my big brother *were* here . . ." On the whole, this is probably a good thing. The only value of having a subjunctive form for these past hypothetical statements is to differentiate between the contrary to fact and the unknown. That is, if you wanted to express a new hypothesis about a noted poet but didn't have access to his childhood medical records, you'd properly say, "If Ezra Pound *was* dyslexic as a child, that would explain some of his strange spelling." However, acting on the wrong belief that *if* has to be followed by the subjunctive, people tend to hypercorrect and say, "If Ezra Pound *were* dyslexic." It is not only jealousy (although it is partly jealousy), and not only my annoyance that the guy's proper name is misrepresented as Da Vinci when it should be Leonardo, that causes me to point out that Dan Brown makes this mistake often in *The Da Vinci Code*, as when a suspicious charcter thinks, "even if it *were* Sophie Neveu, that was hardly a reason to trust her." Should be *was*, Danno.

Some usage books mourn the decline of the past perfect tense—that is, the verb form used in a sentence like "By the time I was eleven, I *had traveled* to England six times"—claiming that people tend to substitute the simple past tense. I don't agree. In fact, I think that a bigger problem is *overuse* of the past perfect. In front of me is the generally unexceptionable grammar text *The Little, Brown Handbook*. Its example for the past perfect is: "The dancer *had trained* in Asia before his performance." I maintain that "The dancer trained in Asia before his performance" is a better and equally clear sentence. Dan Brown is completely flummoxed by the past perfect. He often uses it instead of the past for no discernible reason, and ends up ruining perfectly good sentences. Brown: "Da Vinci had drawn up blueprints for hundreds of inventions he had never built." English: "Leonardo drew up blueprints for hundreds of blueprints he never built."

In the number one spot on the endangered verb form list, I myself would put the imperative mood. This, of course, is the way to express commands or orders. It's traditionally expressed in an inverted second-person present tense, with the *you* understood: "Sweep the floor." (The exception is *to be*, which uses the infinitive form, as in Elmore Leonard's title *Be Cool*.) It is a great mood. Jesus, no less, uses it in Matthew's Gospel addressing God, no less: "Give us this day our daily bread,

and forgive us our trespasses." In our society, which often seems to fear giving offense and always fears law-
suits, this mood is rarely found, other than in the
military, in parochial schools, in traffic signs ("Stop,"
"Walk"), and in innocuous adieus like "Have a good
one" and "Take care." Instead, people use a whole lot of
auxiliaries. That is, if I want you to sweep the floor, I
could utter the sentence, "You _____ sweep the floor,"
and, by placing any of the following in the blank, convey slightly different but immediately understood
meanings: *can*, *could*, *might*, *shall*, *should*, and *will*. I
could also put it in the form of a question like
"Can/could/might/will you sweep the floor?" or a double
question like "Could I ask you to sweep . . . ?" There are
all kinds of other ways people soften commands. Instead of the satisfyingly direct "No Smoking," we have
the presumptuous "Thank You For Not Smoking" or
the loopily existential "There Is No Smoking." Then
there's the word *need*. President George W. Bush said,
"Anybody who harbors terrorists needs to fear the
U.S." Flight attendants would never venture to say,
"Buckle your seat belts, please," but rather remark, "You
need to buckle your seat belts for me" or, less direct
still, "I need you to buckle your seat belts for me." It's
possible to be even less direct than that, and flight

attendants seize the day with "The seat belts need to be fastened."* (There's also the totally indirect, pass-the-buck approach: "The captain has turned on the 'Fasten Seat Belt' sign.") Presumably the fixation on the word *need* comes from psychologist Abraham Maslow's famed hierarchy of needs, but knowing that doesn't make it any more palatable. And in any case, I much prefer the directness you still find on the subways, where you get existential commands that could serve you well in life. On a New York City line I used to ride, the conductor said, "Step lively and watch the closing doors"; in London, it's "Mind the gap."

Even advertisements, which you would think would be loaded with commands, usually shy away from them in favor of declaratives that praise the product ("You're in good hands with Allstate"), butter up the customer ("You deserve a break today"), ask odd questions ("Where's the beef?"), or posit general, almost metaphysical, truths ("Coke is it"). However, the history of advertising contains a few slogans that have dared to

---

* This is an example of a widely used but little-known verb form sometimes called the ergative. It occurs in sentences where what would appear to be the object goes before the verb instead of after it: "The window broke," "This sandwich tastes good," "The car drives nicely," "The order shipped yesterday," or the slogan of Campbell's Chunky line: "Soup that eats like a meal."

command, and I would like to give them a moment in the sun:

"Take it off—take it all off." "Have a Coke and a smile." "Say it with flowers." "Blow some my way" (Chesterfield). "Come to where the flavor is, come to Marlboro country." "Put a tiger in your tank." "Reach out and touch someone." "Be all that you can be." "Dispense with a horse" (Winton Motor Car Company). "Ask the man who owns one" (Packard). "See the U.S.A. in your Chevrolet." "Don't leave home without it." "Go Greyound and leave the driving to us." "Start me up" (Microsoft, after the Rolling Stones). "Just do it." "Guard against intestinal toxicity" (Eno's slogan for its Effervescent Salt, and a personal article of faith for me, even more so than "Step lively and watch the closing doors").

The place where the imperative mood shines is titles of works of art. I guess since the entire world is being addressed, as opposed to one person or a small group, there is no chance of anyone taking offense. In any case, the imperative shows up in films (*Analyze This*), novels (*Look Homeward, Angel*), works of nonfiction (*Steal This Book*), television shows (*Gimme a Break*), comedy albums (the Firesign Theatre's *Don't Crush That Dwarf, Hand Me the Pliers*), and, especially, songs, from "Do the Jerk" to "Love the One You're With."

Command titles form a whole subcategory of Beatles songs: "Come Together," "Get Back," "Don't Let Me Down," "[Give Me] Money," "Give Peace a Chance," "Love Me Do," "Let It Be," "Think for Yourself," and "Help."

For some reason, people with schemes to reform English (and they are legion) often focus on verbs. Possibly the best known of these is C. K. Ogden's Basic English movement of the 1920s and '30s. Intending both to simplify the language and to encourage the use of English as an international second language, Ogden put together a streamlined vocabulary of 850 words that, he contended, were sufficient to convey any nonspecialized meaning. Verbs felt his axe most brutally. In fact, Ogden didn't even accept the word *verbs*; they were included in the category "Operations, etc.," and there were only eighteen of them: *come, get, give, go, keep, let, make, put, seem, take, be, do, have, say, see, send, may,* and *will*. What, you might ask, about such words as *interject, render, infuse, fold, file, plant, immerse,* and *install*? They can all, Ogden says, be replaced by the same two-word phrase: *put in*. Similarly, *assemble* becomes *put together, invent* becomes *make up,* and *photograph* becomes *take pictures*. It's all very ingenious, and Basic attracted some prominent fans, including Winston Churchill and Franklin D. Roosevelt, but its main drawback—an utter inability to convey the subtlety, the complexity, and the poetry of the English language—eventually doomed it to the status of historical curiosity. Even Roosevelt seemed to realize this. In an (unsent) note to Churchill, he wrote, "I wonder what the course of history would have been if in May 1940 you had been able to offer the British people only 'blood, work, eye-water and face-water,' which I understand is the best that Basic can do with five famous words."*

A more recent movement was begun in 1965 by a linguist named D. David Borland. He dubbed it "English-Prime" or "E-Prime," and it consisted of a rather audacious attempt to eliminate from the language the most commonly used verb in it, *to be*. To some extent, this merely took to extremes the traditional and sensible liter-

* Roosevelt was referring, of course, to Churchill's famous (and often misquoted) line, "I have nothing to offer but blood, toil, tears and sweat." Ogden included, without comment, FDR's joke in a 1944 edition of one of his books, but a later editor felt compelled to come to the founder's defense, defensively: "The actual Basic version of Churchill's words, achieved by entering into the spirit and intention of them, would have been more like: 'All I am offering you is death and pain, bitter trouble and hard, unending work." To which one can only offer thanks that Churchill didn't use this bloke as a speechwriter.

ary advice to avoid the passive voice ("Billy was hit by
Tommy") in favor of the active ("Tommy hit Billy") and
to substitute strong verbs ("Johnson owns the store") for
weaker *to be* verbs ("Johnson is the owner of the store").
Getting rid of *to be*, the most irregular of all irregular
verbs, would also presumably delight present and future
English-as-a-second-language students. But Borland and
other E-Prime advocates—who were rooted in the General Semantics movement—were inspired by moral and
philosophical objections to *to be*. Such feelings predate
E-Prime. The philosopher George Santayana wrote in
the 1920s:

> The little word *is* has its tragedies. It names and
> identifies things with the greatest innocence, and
> yet no two are ever identical, and if therein lies the
> charm of wedding them and calling them one,
> therein too lies the danger. Whenever I use the word
> *is*, except in sheer tautology, I deeply misuse it; and
> when I discover my error, the world seems to fall
> asunder.

A current adherent of E-Prime, E. W. Kellogg II, says
that *to be* sentences "confuse one aspect of experience
with a much more complex totality." Can we ever jus-

tifiably say "John is a jerk," or even "The apple is red"? To do so would involve laborious definitions of *jerk* and *red* and would also involve figuring out—apologies to Bill Clinton—what *is* is. E-Prime would also helpfully do away with the currently ubiquitous tautological cliché "It is what it is." The "John is a jerk" example also points to the ease with which the verb lets us throw out value judgments, some of them highly prejudicial, in the guise of objective statements. Kellogg says:

> E-Prime minimizes such presumption, and users must often take overt responsibility for their opinions. For example, "The Northlight is a good restaurant" might become "I enjoy eating at the Northlight restaurant." The unrecognized assumptions that *to be* often introduces can also impair perceptivity and even creativity. For example, compare "The man is drunk" to "The man acts drunk" or "There is no solution to this problem" to "No one has solved this problem yet."

As with so many other grand schemes, one sees the point and also the limitations. In an E-Prime world, Popeye wouldn't have a motto and Hamlet couldn't kick off his most famous soliloquy, nor could he give his ripping rejoinder to his mother: " 'Seems,' madam! nay, it is, I know not 'seems.' "

To be is sometimes omitted for reasons that have nothing to do with philosophy. African American Vernacular English customarily does so with what's called the zero copula—turning the standard English of "It's hot" or "What are you talking about, Willis?" into "It hot" and "What you talking about, Willis?" This is contrary to media caricatures of AAVE, which would render these clauses as "It be hot" and "What you be talking about, Willis?" What scholars call the "invariant habitual *be*" is actually used in highly specific situations, to indicate an ongoing state of affairs ("He be coming over every week") or to provide emphasis. The latter was seen in basketball player Micheal Ray Richardson's famous comment on the fortunes of his team, the New York Knicks: "The ship be sinking."

When people are speaking or writing some form of shorthand, *to be* verbs are usually the first words to go. This definitely saves time and space, and so it's a favorite in headlines ("Bush Elected") and telegrams. It also can have a kind of rough poetry to it. For some reason, I'll always remember a hand-printed sign I once saw next to the change box on a New York City bus: PLEASE DO NOT SHOUT. DRIVER NOT DEAF.

Of course, such omissions carry with them some

risks. Michael Kinsley has amusingly complained about a trend represented by a TV newsreader who looked into the camera and said: "Top government officials adding their voices today to the call for Americans to remain vigilant." Kinsley said the word *adding* here represented a whole new tense, which he called the "gerundiciple." He observed of it:

> The total effect making one dizzy. Past, present, and future melting together as every newsworthy event taking place simultaneously in some dimension beyond the reach of time, where man forever biting dog and yet it remaining news.

Yes, *to be* is a pretty faithful and valuable old friend, and one jettisons it at one's own risk. Once (and if this story isn't true, I don't want to hear about it), Cary Grant received a telegram from a journalist that read. HOW OLD CARY GRANT?

The actor wired back: OLD CARY GRANT FINE. HOW YOU?